SOUTH CHESHIRE COLLEGE

A0063539

New Perspectives on Entrepreneurship

Edited by Fintan Donohue
Principal and CEO
North Hertfordshire College, UK

A collection of interviews and articles reflecting on issues that arise when the entrepreneurial attributes of proactivity, innovativeness and risk-taking are exercised in pursuit of public as well as private value.

The contributors consider the legitimacy of risk-taking in public and social enterprises and the importance of innovation for the public good. They discuss the nature of entrepreneurial leadership and the need to build entrepreneurial organisations, and they confront the necessity of making a virtue out of failure in order to encourage creativity and learning in education, training and the workplace.

The interviewees and authors are drawn from all three sectors, including government, academia and further education, and are from the UK, USA, Ireland and Canada.

D1437750

New Perspectives on Entrepreneurship

Edited by Fintan Donohue

NEW PERSPECTIVES PUBLISHING

Published by
New Perspectives Publishing
Goldsmith Centre for Business
Broadway
Letchworth Garden City
SG6 3GB

Copyright © Fintan Donohue 2011
All rights reserved

ISBN 978-0-9568951-0-3
www.gc4b.com

Acknowledgements

The idea for this book grew out of a research project funded by the Learning and Skills Improvement Service (LSIS). It sought evidence of how creative and entrepreneurial leadership could be applied in public sector organisations to increase productivity and expand market share in a time of reduced public funding. I am grateful for their sponsorship and for the endorsement and support of Caroline Mager who helped me to develop the project. I am also grateful to Tom Bewick who challenged me to think beyond the confines of the original proposal; to Dick Palmer and Richard Thorold who challenged my thinking and contributed to the actions arising out of the research; and to Jan Spaticchia for teaching me much about entrepreneurship.

The interviewees and authors were generous with their time and their ideas and have helped me to develop my thinking around taking risks in pursuit of public value and countenancing failure in pursuit of innovation. I would like to thank my researcher, Kathryn Winter, who carried out the basic research for the project, formulated and carried out the interviews and extracted the key arguments of our academic contributors from their published work. I am lucky in having a superb team at North Hertfordshire College that has been fearless in embracing new ideas, and I would give particular mention to Steve Hollingsworth, Signe Sutherland, Chris McLean, Allan Tyrer and Barbara Briars for their contribution to the thought process.

In expanding the focus of the research from entrepreneurial leadership to entrepreneurial education, I benefited from being invited to several US community colleges and universities to review their entrepreneurship programmes. I would like to thank Bunker Hill and Springfield Colleges, and would like to make particular mention of Janet Strimaitis at Babson College and Jonathan Ortmans and John Courtin at The Kauffman Foundation for introducing me to their inspirational approach to entrepreneurship education.

I would like to thank Vici Cadwallader-Webb and Scott Winter at RSM Tenon for their encouragement, and RSM Tenon for their sponsorship of the publication of this book, and to acknowledge Kate Ling, Hazel Lodge and Kathryn Winter for their work in designing and producing the book.

Finally, a personal thank you to Collette, Erin, Ronan and Ben who gave up their time to make the book possible.

Contributors

Birkinshaw

Julian Birkinshaw
Professor of Strategic and
International Management
London Business School
UK

Fisher

Dame Jackie Fisher
Chief Executive
Newcastle College Group
UK

Casey

Caroline Casey
Social Entrepreneur
Founder of Kanchi
Republic of Ireland

Furdyk

Michael Furdyk
Co-Founder and Director of Technology
TakingITGlobal
Canada

Doel

Martin Doel, OBE
Chief Executive
Association of Colleges
UK

Hall

Lord Hall of Birkenhead, CBE
Chief Executive
Royal Opera House
UK

Donohue

Fintan Donohue
Principal / Chief Executive
North Hertfordshire College
UK

Jones

Peter Jones, CBE
Entrepreneur
Founder of National
Enterprise Academy
UK

Contributors

Morris

Michael H. Morris
N. Malone Mitchell Chair
in Entrepreneurship
Oklahoma State University
USA

Raynor

Andy Raynor
Chief Executive
RSM Tenon
UK

Mulgan

Geoff Mulgan
Chief Executive
Young Foundation
UK

Russell

Geoff Russell
Chief Executive
Skills Funding Agency
UK

Neck

Heidi Neck
Jeffry A. Timmons Professor
of Entrepreneurial Studies
Babson College
USA

Ortmans

Jonathan Ortmans
President, Global Entrepreneurship Week
Senior Fellow, Ewing Marion Kauffman Foundation
USA

Contents

Contents

innovation

continual

Most of what you hear about **entrepreneurship** is all wrong. **It's not magic;** **it's not** **mysterious;** and it has nothing to do with genes. **It's a discipline** and, like any other discipline, **it can** **be learned.**

Peter Drucker, 1994

Note on the editor

Fintan Donohue is Principal and CEO of North Hertfordshire College. He has a degree in Law and an MPhil in Change Management and has worked extensively in the private sector as an adviser on organisational development and change management. He is an experienced Board member, having held ten non-executive posts since 1990. He is an elected member of both the Learning and Skills Improvement Service (LSIS) Council and the Association of Colleges (AoC) Board of Corporation. As an adviser to the London Organising Committee of the Olympic Games and the Home Office on the Bridging the Gap Olympic Games project, he is at the forefront of a changed agenda for the FE sector. He is the author of several published articles on leadership, creativity and learner-led organisational development and was the lead Principal adviser to BECTA on technology and innovation for leaders in the public sector. He has most recently published research on the personalisation of leadership in the FE sector. He is an AoC Skills Champion for several industries and is the first Principal in the sector to be appointed FE Ambassador to a Sector Skills Council. His most recent work on the role of entrepreneurship in a changing public sector is breaking new ground and is challenging those who lead in the further education sector to reinvent their curricula for a different future.

Introduction

When I started investigating the value of entrepreneurial leadership in the public sector, I anticipated finding evidence to support my belief that we needed to rethink the way we developed leadership within public sector organisations. I did not, however, anticipate finding evidence for the strategic importance of entrepreneurship to so many organisations. I certainly didn't anticipate that the findings would act as a catalyst for change and a beacon of hope for a generation of students in our colleges.

The contributors to this book have shared their views on what it means to exercise entrepreneurial leadership across all sectors. They analyse the value of organisations adopting an entrepreneurial orientation and they consider the importance of inspiring an entrepreneurial mindset in our schools and colleges. Michael H. Morris describes the three key dimensions of entrepreneurial attitudes and behaviours as proactiveness, innovativeness and risk-taking. The exercise of these attributes is not, he says, an either/or determination but a question of degree and frequency. He presents a definition of entrepreneurship that makes it easy to argue for its relevance in every walk of life and prompted me to think about how I could apply all this learning about the entrepreneurial mindset to the Further Education sector.

I found some of the answers at Babson College in Massachusetts. Babson believe they have created an educational environment that fosters "continual innovation, fearless experimentation, and structured chaos". It is, says Heidi Neck, about method rather than content—about the way you learn being as important as what you learn. While Babson teaches aspiring entrepreneurs in a higher education setting, I believe they have pioneered a way of learning that can afford all students a head-start in employment whether they wish to be self-employed, start a business or add value to an existing enterprise.

As children we are naturally creative and fearless; but then we enter secondary education and fearless experimentation makes way for fear of failure. Michael Furdyk believes that the secondary curriculum is testing the creativity out of students and disenfranchising their teachers and that this is damaging and very difficult to reverse. The obsession with failure as an entirely negative concept has significant implications for the problems that confront us. Innovation in education, enterprise and public services is of paramount importance to our well-being, and if we are going to try something new we are not always going to get it right first time. Peter Jones says that we have to reframe failure as feedback—as a learning tool in pursuit of a better product or an enhanced service. In a similar vein, Caroline Casey discusses failure as an investment in learning, arguing that if you don't sanction failure within your organisation you won't benefit from the innate creativity of your team.

Another word that causes consternation in the public sector is risk—but that, too, is part of the equation. Risk is a prerequisite for innovation just as failure is a possible outcome. Julian Birkinshaw and Geoff Mulgan believe that the real risk to public services is the damage done when risk is avoided in pursuit of short term success and long-term career prospects. Birkinshaw discusses it in terms of errors of omission and commission, arguing that the former are often made because they are less injurious to the career of a public servant than the latter. Mulgan develops the argument in favour of incentives for risk-taking behaviour: "Bureaucracies lack the competitive spur that drives businesses to create new products and services. Their rules squeeze out anything creative or original. Their staff are penalised for mistakes but never rewarded for taking successful risks."

The Ewing Marion Kauffman Foundation in Missouri, the world's largest foundation devoted to entrepreneurship, recognises the global significance of entrepreneurship. The Kauffman Foundation together with Enterprise UK co-founded Global Entrepreneurship Week. Jonathan Ortmans, who led the initiative on behalf of Kauffman, is unequivocal about its importance: "To rise out of our current economic and social difficulties, we need entrepreneurs to innovate and take risks." Entrepreneurs, he says, create value, fuel economic growth, create jobs and raise living standards. Both Ortmans and Neck are strong believers in entrepreneurship as a positive force for social change; but Europe, according to Peter Jones, is at a disadvantage here. There is a cultural divide between the US and Europe which is often characterised as the 'I can' attitude of Americans against the more conversative 'can I?' attitude of Europeans. Peter Jones is committed to changing this and he believes that Further Education has a significant role to play in making it happen.

When a small group of Principals[1] started thinking about the benefits of an entrepreneurial orientation for their colleges and their students, it was clear that we were heading for difficult times; however, the sheer scale of the economic downturn had not yet been fully realised. It is now apparent that while qualifications still have an innate value, they have limited purchase in a changing economy. This has prompted Geoff Russell to call for college Principals—"some of the best education business managers in the country"—to shift their focus from qualifications to the qualities that will best prepare students to add immediate value to their own careers, to local businesses and to the wider community. In a similar vein, Andy Raynor believes that the college experience itself should be a catalyst for entrepreneurial ambition.

Looking at the sector as a whole, it is clear that college leaders no longer have the option of hiding behind the security of a qualification system, a pedagogy and a curriculum framework that was built for an era of certainty, industrialisation, localism and compliance. The sector needs to be transformed and we need to follow the example of Jackie Fisher in counterbalancing commercialism and entrepreneurship with responsible stewardship in order to maximise the public resources we enjoy. Martin Doel recognises that many FE principals are skilled and confident in the exercise of entrepreneurial leadership and that the sector is ready for this transformation.

[1] Matt Atkinson, Amarjit Basi, Di Dale, Sally Dicketts, Nigel Leigh, Stella Mbubaegbu, Maureen Mellor, Dick Palmer, Marion Plant, Richard Thorold.

There is much in the Further Education curriculum that lends itself to a more enterprising model. While Tony Hall describes people who work in the arts as natural entrepreneurs—innovators and risk takers who continually test the boundaries of their physical, psychological and artistic limits—even our creative arts students remain constrained by the tyranny of the timetable and a syllabus designed by an entrenched awarding body. We need to make changes that will allow our students to thrive in structured chaos on campuses that concentrate on learning rather than teaching, immersed in what Babson College refers to as an entrepreneurial 'living laboratory'.

Together with other Principals in the sector, I do not believe that our current structure and practices will enable us to make the radical shift that accompanies an entrepreneurial orientation. In the final section of this book, we present the case for like-minded colleges to come together and create new entities—a combination of private sector autonomy and public sector values—to align innovation, curriculum, technology and growth. These entities will allow us to build entrepreneurship into every product, course and experience that the organisation touches. It will be an enterprise tasked with advancing entrepreneurial thought and action in colleges and in the public sector organisations that choose to embrace entrepreneurship as a strategic partner.

By sharing their experiences of entrepreneurship and their views on the importance of entrepreneurial education, the contributors to this book have made the case for some colleges to become visibly entrepreneurial—to become colleges where people choose to learn in a different way and with a focus on destination rather than qualification. It is a transformation predicated upon our clear sense of obligation as stewards of the public purse, our staff and our students, together with a commitment to reinvest our successes and our profits in favour of our colleges and the communities we serve.

It is clear that college leaders no longer have the option of hiding behind the security of a qualification system, a pedagogy and a curriculum framework that was built for an era of certainty, industrialisation, localism and compliance.

Fintan Donohue, 2011

Introduction

perspective

a global

An article by

Jonathan Ortmans

President, Global Entrepreneurship Week

Senior Fellow, Ewing Marion Kauffman Foundation

A global renaissance for entrepreneurship

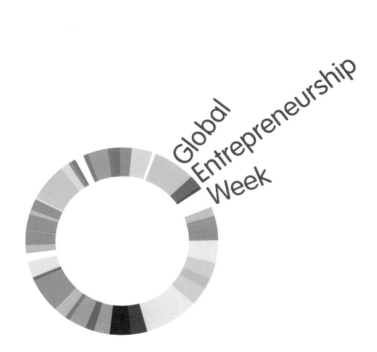

❝TO RISE OUT OF OUR CURRENT ECONOMIC AND SOCIAL DIFFICULTIES, WE NEED ENTREPRENEURS TO INNOVATE AND TAKE RISKS ❞

Ortmans

The past two years have presented historic challenges, but also opportunities, for entrepreneurial minds. By seeking solutions to the pressing financial problems, as well as to the growing environmental and social challenges of our time, entrepreneurs around the world have come up with more innovative ideas than ever for new products and faster, cheaper and better ways of doing things. That is what entrepreneurs do. They create value, fueling economic growth, creating jobs and raising income and living standards as they succeed.

This is why, facing unemployment and growth stagnation effects of the economic crisis, national leaders, scrambling for policies to break away from these effects, have increasingly moved entrepreneurship to the center of their conversations about the economy. From President Obama's recent Startup America Partnership (an alliance intended to dramatically increase the development, prevalence and success of new innovative, high-growth U.S. firms) to Prime Minister Cameron's own Startup Britain initiative, they are acting in practical terms in promoting a culture that applauds new firm formation. They have taken a closer look at data demonstrating that in the world's biggest economy, the United States, young firms are indisputably the most effective source of new jobs.

For example, research has shown that on average between 1977 and 2005, existing firms were net job destroyers, losing one million jobs net combined per year, while new firms added an average of three million jobs in their first year. Simply put, net job growth occurs in the U.S. economy only through startup firms. Moreover, during recessionary years, job creation at startups remains stable, while net job losses at existing firms are highly sensitive to the business cycle.[1] Entrepreneurs have indeed led the way to recovery from previous economic downturns by seeding new ideas and creating jobs. More than half of the companies on the 2009 U.S. Fortune 500 list were launched during a recession or bear market.[2]

"EVERY NATION SHOULD SCRUTINIZE ITS POLICY ENVIRONMENT TO LOOK FOR BARRIERS TO ENTREPRENEURSHIP WHETHER IN TAX REGULATIONS OR THE EDUCATION SYSTEM"

Also interesting is the finding that enterprises that eventually generate a billion dollars or more in revenue will fuel economic growth and job creation for many years, and ultimately will spawn the next generation of entrepreneurs and innovators. Recent research has estimated that about 15 of these companies arise every year in the United States, and if that number rose to somewhere between 30 and 60, the United States would increase its growth rate by one percent, meaning GDP would double in 18 years versus 24, and incomes would rise commensurately.[3]

These are just some examples of data from one economy, but it is common for leaders from many countries to no longer think of new business creation as mere adjunct players on the sidelines of our economies but as central to their well-functioning. The recognition of entrepreneurs as the lifeblood of

[1]Kane, Tim. *The Importance of Startups in Job Creation and Job Destruction.* The Ewing Marion Kauffman Foundation. 2010.
[2]Stangler, Dane. *The Economic Future Just Happened.* The Ewing Marion Kauffman Foundation. 2009.
[3]Litan, Robert. *Inventive Billion Dollar Firms: A Faster Way to Grow.* The Ewing Marion Kauffman Foundation. 2010.

growing economies has fortunately translated into concrete reforms to build a legal and regulatory environment conducive to entrepreneurship. For example, we saw UK Chancellor George Osborne exempt employers from a proportion of National Insurance Contributions for the first ten jobs they create (except in London, the South East and East of England). Perhaps one of the most unique policy events of the past year was President Obama´s Presidential Summit on Entrepreneurship when the White House, keen to promote economic stability around the world, hosted a Summit focused only on "global" entrepreneurship with almost all the guests from outside the United States. This was a political risk in a climate in which so many Americans, anxious about their local economy, are blinded to the vital role entrepreneurs play in building the stable economies overseas essential to our growing firms at home. And the summit will continue with Prime Minister Erdogan from Turkey offering to take the baton and host the next Global Summit on Entrepreneurship.

Entrepreneurs can only flourish where they have strong support networks. The above examples of initiatives were possible because entrepreneurs have been set apart from some of the negative perceptions of big business and the blame being placed on large financial institutions for the economic meltdown. The most common problem, however, is the rejection of failure. Although a stigmatized "condition" in many cultures, failure is an inevitable part of the process as much as risk-taking and creative-thinking. The aim is to bring something new to the marketplace, sometimes creating a whole new source of demand. And with all attempts at innovating or doing something that no one else has before, comes the possibility of failing or, as I prefer to describe it, recycling the ideas and teams forming to develop them.

Creating cultural capital for entrepreneurs is clearly the hardest part of renewed efforts to drive up productivity. It is an intangible, cultural shift that is very hard for governments and other leaders to stimulate. This is where the Global Entrepreneurship Week (GEW) movement has contributed in an enormous way.

In over 100 countries, GEW has combed for nascent entrepreneurs, financiers, mentors, role models and other crucial supporters. Perhaps a testament to that, young potential entrepreneurs around the world no longer look just to traditional rock star entrepreneurs like Bill Gates and Steve Jobs, but to new heroes of the global technological revolution like China's Robin Li of Baidu and Ghana's Chinery-Hesse, an early investor in the Internet cafes which have given thousands of Ghanaians access to information and global connections. With each passing year, GEW has seen the building of a worldwide culture of innovation and entrepreneurship through the more than 20 million people who engage in Global Entrepreneurship Week activities. In addition to the ever-increasing numbers of active participants in GEW events, a growing number of individuals and organizations are collaborating on planning activities that nurture the startup community. In November 2010, the number of partner organizations had climbed to 23,952, while volunteer hours dedicated to GEW activities eclipsed 64,000.

While commitment from policymakers and grassroots efforts such as GEW are all contributing to the building of a more entrepreneurial global economy, succeeding at entrepreneurship will never come down to a formula. There is no single cleanly-packaged framework to follow, and nations should be careful to adopt strategies, not plans, in order to preserve the inherently messy nature of entrepreneurial capitalism. Every nation, though, should scrutinize its policy environment to look for barriers to entrepreneurship whether in tax regulations or the education system. For example, Europeans have less to gain from taking business risks as a consequence of the relatively higher tax rates, and much more to lose because of more punitive attitudes to bankruptcy. In the United States, it is the absence of a high skilled immigration policy which could, for example, provide startup visas, that hinders the creation of new high impact firms.

Entrepreneurship experts in the U.S. have found serious barriers to the commercialization of new products, even when ambitious founders very often succeed at showing that their product works and is desired by the market. This problem is particularly common at U.S. research universities, a sad reality given the heavy concentration of scientists and researchers and the heavy investment in university research.[4] Education is another area in which the U.S. continues to struggle.[5] So far, at the primary and secondary level, there is little encouragement of creativity, entrepreneurial thinking or opportunity recognition.

In the manner described through these examples, policymakers will find ways to connect more innovators with capital, more aspiring entrepreneurs with mentors, and more innovations with markets. The commanding question should be: How can we encourage more innovation in processes, creative thinking, risk-taking and an entrepreneurial culture that has more citizens of a nation ferreting out better ways of doing things? Entrepreneurship, especially high-growth, high-impact entrepreneurship, emerges when the proper incentive structure is in place, when individual initiative is encouraged, and when individuals have the opportunity to engage in innovation.

Each economic policy action should move us toward those goals. To rise out of our current economic and social difficulties, we need entrepreneurs to innovate and take risks. Not all of them will succeed, but the more we tap into the world's human talent, the higher the chances that we will see more high-impact success.

---

[4]The Ewing Marion Kauffman Foundation. *Rules for Growth: Promoting Innovation and Growth Through Legal Reform*. 2011.
[5]The Ewing Marion Kauffman Foundation. *On the Road to an Entrepreneurial Economy: A Research and Policy Guide*, Version 2.0. 2007.

enterp

the entrepreneur

An article by

Peter Jones, CBE

Entrepreneur, Founder of National Enterprise Academy

*Reclaiming entrepreneurship
for the public space*

" WE NEED TO SHATTER THE MYTH THAT ENTREPRENEURS ARE ONLY IN IT FOR THEMSELVES AND RECLAIM THE WORD FOR THE PUBLIC SPACE "

Jones

I'm not a teacher, nor am I an expert in education. I do, however, believe I have something to offer the education system. Why? Well, I'm an employer and understand the qualities we need from our future workforce. I'm also a successful entrepreneur and I want to use my knowledge to nurture Britain's entrepreneurial talent.

I want to help young people and young enterprise to flourish. With the unprecedented changes in our economy, our society, and the ongoing efficiencies being sought; now, more than ever, college leaders need to be entrepreneurial and create entrepreneurial organisations in order to deliver what is being asked of them.

In 2009, my National Enterprise Academy (NEA) opened its doors to students aged 16 to 19 in Amersham and in Manchester. I have big plans for scaling it up so that it rolls-out nationwide and offers thousands of courses to students all over Britain. I love my work with the NEA and it gives me huge pleasure to use the profile that I have achieved through television to try and make a difference—encouraging, nurturing and supporting entrepreneurial activity.

When asked about leadership and enterprise within the further education system, I don't believe there is a 'one size fits all' approach. Tutors and principals from an education background are very well placed to understand the needs of their students. I do believe, however, that colleges need to become hubs of entrepreneurial action in the provision they offer, the staff and leadership they employ, and the culture and environment they create.

We have a situation right now where 50% of Brits would prefer to be self-employed, according to the latest EU Entrepreneurship survey, but only 6.8% of the UK population expect to start a business in the next 3 years.[1] The two main issues preventing this are fear of failure (38% of people in the UK would be reluctant to start a company due to fear of failure) and a lack of confidence in their skills.

The FE system trains 3 million people every year, so has a huge responsibility for helping to create a more enterprising UK. Entrepreneurial leaders and enterprising colleges are vital. For me, this is not about a leader or college principal having a specific list of jobs on their CV. It's about a mindset and whether they have the attributes needed to run a commercially successful business.

I have a list of ten things that I believe are needed in order to be a successful entrepreneur, and I don't see why leading a college requires a different mindset to running a large telecoms company or a coffee shop. Indeed, the sorts of budgets college leaders have to deal with will exceed that of many businesses. The ambitions and outcomes may vary, as will their ability to deliver all ten of these attributes, but the end result needs to be success: Success in terms of giving students the best learning environment and preparing them for employment; and, crucially in this age, doing it within budget. Let's take a closer look at my list of attributes and see how they apply to the further education sector.

The first is **vision.** If you dream, dream big. In the National Enterprise Academy we dream big for the academy and we dream big for our students.

[1] Eurobarometer (2007), *Entrepreneurship Survey of the EU (25 Member States), United States, Iceland and Norway*, p. 7, http://ec.europa.eu/enterprise/policies/sme/files/survey/eurobarometer2007/eb2007report_en.pdf

We allow them to have aspirations and to follow their dreams. The best college principals have a clear vision that inspires their staff. Sheffield College is an example of where enterprise is at the heart of their vision.

Number two is **influence.** Every entrepreneur needs others at some point. In a college environment this means education specialists and business leaders collaborating to bring their skills together to benefit the student. Richmond Adult and Community College is a great example of an influential college, placing enterprise at the centre of their role within the local community. Number three is **confidence** and having an inner self-belief. I really believe there is no such thing as failure—only feedback. A college culture and attitude to risk must reflect this.

Number four is **commitment,** where action follows decisions. The college principal and management team must be empowered to make decisions; so, too, should learners, with genuine opportunities for them to get involved. At number five, entrepreneurs need to be **results-orientated.** In education, this has too often been about testing—hitting the target but missing the point. At the NEA, we put energy and focus into ensuring that our students are entrepreneurial and able to put those skills to good use when they leave, ideally as entrepreneurs or as valued employees.

Timing, number six, is key for any leader; not just in business but in life too—their own health and support from their partner or family is crucial to success. **Perseverance** is at number seven. Successful entrepreneurs have determination and persistence, and leaders in education need to have the determination to overcome bureaucracy, cope with continual change and introduce new initiatives. At eight is the need to be **caring**: to understand the needs and wants of your people. In a college environment, this means listening to your staff, your governors and, don't forget, your students! Next up is **action** at number nine. Entrepreneurs want to make things happen. They don't just go through the motions. They don't do the minimum required. They throw themselves into a situation and make it work.

Jones

Last but not least is **intuition**. Good leaders and entrepreneurs instinctively follow their gut feelings to make great decisions.

Entrepreneurial leadership exists at all levels of an organisation and I would encourage the principal to bring in partners and staff who have these attributes. There are entrepreneurs in your building and on your Board of Corporation who have plenty to offer. It's never too late to develop enterprise skills and talents, so colleges must factor this in to development and training. There is no better (and cheaper!) way to do this than by inviting local entrepreneurs along to inspire staff and students.

Culturally, there is a stark difference in the entrepreneurial mindset between the UK and the US. Here, there tends to be a 'can I?' approach; whereas, in the US, an 'I can' attitude is instilled from an early age. Colleges are uniquely placed to help address this cultural gap with their relationships with local communities and businesses and their proximity to the vocational demands of our economy. They should become the entrepreneurial hubs of their community as the demand for entrepreneurial support intensifies and we seek new ways to create jobs in our economy.

So, in conclusion, what can be done to promote this entrepreneurial mindset and develop our students? Well, firstly, methods of enterprise teaching need to be urgently reviewed. Some people are more entrepreneurial than others, but I am positive that you can teach someone to be an entrepreneur.

At the NEA we give students access to real businesses and the challenges they face. We bring business into the classroom and we take students out into the business world via work experience placements. These placements go beyond the traditional work experience of sweeping up hair or making the tea. We spend time with the employers to ensure that they are offering our students a realistic experience.

I would like to see further education become synonymous with entrepreneurship, particularly through the vocational courses they offer. Colleges are well placed to help individuals learn about specific trades and sectors and about the broader principals of business.

In fact, I'm sure many tutors have entrepreneurial ventures on the side. I want to see more colleges place real enterprise and entrepreneurship at the heart of their added-value, and develop strategies to plug gaps in current approaches.

Finally, entrepreneurial leadership in the sector needs to be developed and enhanced. Public and civic leaders are already entrepreneurial—spotting opportunities, marshalling resources, and creating business solutions; yet I fear that for too many in the public sector, the word entrepreneur continues to be somewhat of a 'dirty word'.

We need to shatter the myth that entrepreneurs are only in it for themselves and to reclaim the word for the public space. This can be supported by raising the priority of entrepreneurial education in professional development. We could open up teaching networks to business owners and entrepreneurs who have great ideas and want to

"GOOD LEADERS AND ENTREPRENEURS INSTINCTIVELY FOLLOW THEIR GUT FEELINGS TO MAKE GREAT DECISIONS"

make a difference. And we could reward those principals who are really making an entrepreneurial difference and inspire others to follow suit.

Who knows, if we could do all of this we might even see some principals leave their jobs and end up on a future series of *Dragon's Den*. Then we'll know we're getting somewhere!

An interview with

Andy Raynor

Chief Executive, RSM Tenon

The accidental entrepreneur

"WE SHOULD STOP BEING FEARFUL OF THE WORD 'ENTREPRENEUR' AND LOOK AT WHAT LIES BEHIND IT"

Raynor

The classic view of entrepreneurs is that they are of the 'bright spark' variety in pursuit of a great idea, or that they have been ambitious for business success from a young age. But many choose self-employment or to run their own business in order to make the best of a downturn.

In the workplace, says Andy Raynor, there are two choices. You work for yourself or you work for somebody else. Many entrepreneurs choose the former only when the latter ceases to be viable. Either that, or they stumble across an unmet demand or happen upon a credible opportunity. So, irrespective of whether entrepreneurs are born or made, many people simply find themselves running a business.

The qualities that then differentiate the entrepreneur from the workaday business owner are staying power and a positive attitude towards change. Entrepreneurs always ask two questions. They ask 'why?' and they ask 'what's next?'. They ask why, not to be capricious but to learn and to understand and to be best placed to make a judgement. And they ask what's next because today is no longer an issue for them—it's all about tomorrow. Entrepreneurs, says Raynor, do this intuitively: "If you ask an entrepreneur what's next, you might as well put the kettle on and make yourself comfortable because you're going to be there for sometime!"

Entrepreneurs are also control freaks — a quality that works both for and against them. In the early days, it makes them tenacious and resilient; qualities needed by people who never take no for an answer. But once they've rewritten the rules and the business is up and running, they find themselves constrained by the rules of their own making; and, worse than that, they have to work with other people!

"I have sat in front of entrepreneurs", says Raynor, "spitting feathers because their senior managers just don't get it—and you have to explain to them that only a small proportion of people in the workplace share their attitude towards work." Even so, they find it hard to relate to people who are not willing to work hard and make personal sacrifices, and who are incapable of exercising sound commercial judgement. They make the mistake of believing that they need to surround themselves with 'rainmakers' when what they really need is a balanced team.

It is critical for entrepreneurs to recognise when their management skills need to be augmented or they will become a negative influence on the business. Raynor understands that this is a difficult transition requiring significant self-discipline: "When you have started with nothing and have had all the responsibility on your shoulders—when you've wandered around the garden wondering whether or not you still own your house—well, that's a very hard thing to deal with."

Nonetheless, entrepreneurs are rarely finishers. Not only do they inhabit tomorrow, they already inhabit the next project or the next big idea. They need someone to sweep up after them. They tend not to go looking for talent—that isn't within their purview—but they are very quick to spot it and tend to have a positive attitude towards the abilities of other people, especially when it's in their own interest. "I have never", says Raynor, "come across an entrepreneur in a successful business who saw talent as a threat."

Conventional wisdom also views entrepreneurs as 'punters'—risk-takers in search of short term gain. The reality, according to Raynor, is quite different: "They put enormous effort into mitigating risk and they cast their net wide in order to learn as much as they can before they make a decision."

What people on the outside see as a risk, entrepreneurs see as a considered business judgement with a likelihood of success. They are 'sponges' when it comes to information or advice. They tend to have a deep rather than broad knowledge of their own sector, and they are quick to seek out and benefit from the advice of those who have been there before.

This view of the entrepreneur—of their personal characteristics and business practices—calls into question the value of continuing to debate whether or not entrepreneurial leadership belongs in the public sector. It tells us to stop being fearful of the word 'entrepreneur' and to look at what lies behind it. Private sector entrepreneurs are marked by staying power, resourcefulness, creativity, a positive attitude towards change and relentless efforts to mitigate risk. These are characteristics, says Raynor, that are entirely interchangeable with the public sector.

The real debate should not be about the value of entrepreneurial leadership but about how the sector can be transformed to empower and celebrate innovative local managers. Any public service manager intent on not taking 'no' for an answer needs his or her stakeholders to say 'yes'; not to hide behind a 'that's not the way we do things around here' mentality. This is not just a problem for the public sector, says Raynor. It is a problem for any large organisation. Of necessity, they have a series of tramlines which people have to go down. The larger they get, the more institutionalised they get. This forces them to look outside for new ideas and innovation because they are no longer capable of creating the conditions that will generate internal entrepreneurs.

Raynor

Entrepreneurs also have an eye to the long-term—a characteristic perfectly suited to the public sector and in the interests of all its stakeholders; but one which is likely to be stymied by the top down targets which have consistently driven the sector to the short-term. Added to that is the heavy hand of accountability, the result of which Raynor likens to increased regulation in his own world of financial services: "A tick-box attitude to quality doesn't improve people's judgement. It allows you to demonstrate well what you may be doing badly, and encourages an approach that maximises evidence rather than quality."

In the private sector, he says, you are encouraged to do something brilliantly well and there is sufficient latitude for you to exercise your own judgement. The public sector, with its rigid line management and unyielding objectives, could nurture mediocrity: "Public sector managers inhabit a world in which personal judgement—often subjective and intuitive—has no time to play itself out. They spend their time accounting for what they're doing and why they're doing it, when they just need to be getting on with it and applying all their skills and know-how to adapting and changing as circumstances demand."

There is a huge divide in the workforce, says Raynor, between those who are negative or passive in response to change and those who react by seeking solutions and opportunities. It is this latter attitude that he would like to see instilled in students and apprentices. The learning environment, he says, should be a place where people can try, fail, learn from their mistakes and turn things around—where they can explore and develop their creative abilities and discover that they are capable of being more than passive recipients of change. There will be those who will thrive and those who will enjoy the learning experience but not be inclined to take it any further and that, says Raynor, is perfectly OK.

"THE COLLEGE EXPERIENCE ITSELF SHOULD BE A CATALYST FOR ENTREPRENEURIAL AMBITION"

An important aspect of this kind of education, and a challenge for college Principals, is to make those values part of the whole college experience: "You need to create an environment and a community which is visibly and viscerally entrepreneurial—where people can immerse themselves in creativity and innovation and just soak it up. The college experience itself should be a catalyst for entrepreneurial ambition."

Raynor offers his own measure of success for further and higher education. Business school graduates, he says, frequently enter the commercial world and remark that it is not at all what they expected: "Wouldn't it be wonderful if students, business or otherwise, entered the workplace and found it to be exactly as they had anticipated—a world that they already understood and where they could create immediate value for themselves or their employers."

One way to achieve this is to bring business leaders and entrepreneurs into the classroom; but entrepreneurs aren't entrepreneurs forever: "There are people still doing it, who are thrilled by what they're doing and who make you want to follow them out of the room! And there are people who can tell you what they've done but are no longer in the moment. You need the former. You may not have heard of them but they will light up any classroom."

Raynor

creativity

the public sector

An interview with

Lord Hall of Birkenhead, CBE

Chief Executive, Royal Opera House

This wonderful, mad world of opera!

"ENTREPRENEURIALISM IS AT THE HEART OF A CULTURAL ORGANISATION... ARTISTS ARE NATURAL ENTREPRENEURS"

Hall

The adoption of an entrepreneurial approach to public sector leadership is fraught with issues of legitimacy; and when the public sector in question is arts and culture, the leader has to deal with the legitimacy of the organisation per se and not just his or her own management style and attitude to risk.

Tony Hall joined the Royal Opera House from the BBC in 2001. His first impression was that "there was an awful lot that was right and there were some things that were wrong, and much of what was wrong was that the place had no legitimacy". While he had no problem with its

artistic ambition outstripping its financial capabilities—"that should be the case with any decent cultural organisation"—he believed that the organisation simply wasn't commercial enough.

He also wanted to redress the balance between public funding and public access: "To put it bluntly, if you are taking a proportion—and at that point it was well over 40%— of your turnover from grant, then you have to reach as many people as you can who would want to consume something from you."

Legitimacy was also at issue in managing the delicate balance between finding the widest possible audience for opera and ballet—often in its more traditional form—and experimenting with the form to deliver something very expensive to a very much smaller audience of artists and enthusiasts. Hall reframes this argument in terms of the responsibility of the Royal Opera House to develop the art form: "Why would you pay £28m for us if we weren't taking risks?"

Needing to confront issues of legitimacy on several fronts, Hall felt that the politics of running a public organisation should be the least of them: "You have to get the debate away from management and on to why you exist, and that's for the art. You have to be entrepreneurial because you want to bring in new people in innovatory ways to understand what drives you and what makes opera and ballet such wonderful art forms—and you want to excite people."

Hall spent his handover period getting a feel for the "warp and weft and flow" of the organisation and trying to understand what the organisation was about and what it was trying to do: "It meant talking to people and working at a pace and in a way that people understood." This, he believes, is a more difficult—"less explosive"—but fundamentally better way to bring about change.

He brought the Finance and Human Resources roles, previously staffed by consultants, in-house; and he reorientated the highly successful capital-raising team to apply their efforts to revenue-raising: "I had to do these things in the first three months—no messing about." He was facing a deficit of £2m in his first year, growing to a deficit of £8.5m by the third year and there was no proper system for seeing what they were spending month-on-month or predicting costs going forward: "You have to remember that you have fixed costs committed 3-5 years ahead in this bonkers, wonderful, financially mad world of opera."

In this same period, Hall did something that people found really difficult to understand. He realised that the House could be about more than the main stage. There were other performance spaces – the Linbury Studio Theatre and the ballet rehearsal spaces – and they could be utilised to address issues of both financial and artistic legitimacy: "They offered a fantastic opportunity for us to take risks—our own version of a BBC2 or BBC4 working alongside BBC1—a place for artists to take risks and to add to the art form; a place for new talent and the potential for new audiences."

He established RoH2 to take risks, to innovate, to do for ballet and opera the things they couldn't do for themselves: "Externally it may not seem much but internally it was huge because the place was bi-polar and suddenly here was this third arm". This radical move, however, of openly sanctioning innovation—of creating a safe place to take risks away from the main stage—had a wholly positive result on the ballet and theatre companies and they started coming up with their own ideas about how they could do things differently.

Once he had put the senior management team and RoH2 in place, Hall didn't have to inculcate an entrepreneurial spirit in the organisation. Entrepreneurialism, he says, is at the heart of a cultural organisation. Artists are natural entrepreneurs. They are proactive and innovative, and risk is inherent in the development of their art. They continually challenge the boundaries of their physical, psychological and artistic limits. Furthermore, the teams that collaborate on a production have to be creative, flexible and comfortable with risk.

Hall is particularly interested in the entrepreneurial team— the diverse people, sometimes strangers to each other, who come together, work under extraordinary pressures of time and resources to deliver an opera, a ballet or a current affairs broadcast, and then disband and start again with a new project and a new team. At the critical moment—at the moment of performance— they're on their own: "What can I do?" says Hall. "You rely on a whole range of people to problem-solve and get things right. It's not a bank. They haven't got time to come to me".

With his own team in place, Hall started to run things differently. It struck him that the place was somewhat monarchical. He likes people to know what is going on; so he shared financial information, involved people in pricing decisions and kept them apprised of how the season was going. The development of a commercial arm was a slower process but one that was essential to the success of the organisation. He refutes the argument that great things are produced when money is tight: "That's rubbish," he says. "You're thinking about how to pay the bills. There is no development."

"THE JOB OF AN ENTREPRENEURIAL LEADER OF A CULTURAL ORGANISATION IS TO ENABLE PEOPLE TO DO THE THINGS THEY WANT TO DO"

He started with the basics: "We knew how to sell tickets." An early commercial venture was to rent the House to the eclectic singer-composer Björk. It was done to make money and the press "had a field day" but, he says, "she was interesting—experimental—so it felt OK". It stretched the envelope of what the Royal Opera House did and it was a big statement early in his tenure. He has subsequently bought a DVD company, relayed performances into cinemas and on to big screens, developed 'video on demand' and produced *Carmen* in 3D.

Whilst revenue-raising in its own right, it was also aimed at bringing people to the Royal Opera House: "If your first chance of getting to see and to understand opera is sitting in a cinema, in a more 'natural' environment, you might well decide to come here." He also recognises that to attract new audiences you need to understand how people consume media and how they consume the arts. Today, that requires an engagement with social media and that means empowering younger people to make decisions: "I understand social media intellectually but not viscerally. There is a big gap. It's not part of my life."

So, the RoH Facebook site came directly from his online team who subsequently invited the Facebook members to drinks at the Royal Opera House and "Hey Presto!", he says, "we found ourselves with one hundred new members who had not come to an opera before". Similarly, the idea for the 'Twitter' opera came from RoH2; from the people who understood it: "What it pointed to was a new form of creativity in an online world. Opera Magazine reported that we'd lost our marbles; but it worked and it was fun."

The Royal Opera House operates by looking 3-5 years ahead, making judgments about what the revenues and costs will be and then looking again every six months. It's all, says Hall, about balancing risk. It's about weaving together artists and material to bring in revenue from traditionalists and enthusiasts and new audiences alike. You need 'bankers', you need names, you need novelty, you need experiment and you need overlap.You might need a name to bring audiences back to a familiar production and you might need reduced price seats to encourage audiences to 'take a risk' with something new: "The whole season becomes a balancing out of risks, including last minute decisions to cope

with illness and injury. There are a whole lot of things that can go wrong. You're living on the edge."

Hall believes that the job of an entrepreneurial leader of a cultural organisation is to enable people to do the things they want to do. But, notwithstanding the strengths and abilities of the people in the organisation today, he believes that an enabling culture cannot survive a less 'entrepreneurial' outlook on leadership: "I've seen organisations that have changed overnight because somebody came in and said, no, I want to control this."

The Royal Opera House, he says, has weathered the recession to date because it's taken risks: "We haven't become 'The National Tosca House'. We've put in all sorts of exciting things on all sorts of stages, getting things out to people and creating a buzz around it. You've got to carry on taking risks because the worst thing you can do at a time of recession is to go bland."

Hall

An extract from the work of

Michael H. Morris

N. Malone Mitchell Chair in Entrepreneurship,
Oklahoma State University

'Entrepreneurship in established organisations: the case of the public sector'

❝ A COMPANY'S ENTREPRENEURIAL ORIENTATION IS POSITIVELY ASSOCIATED WITH NUMEROUS MEASURES OF CORPORATE PERFORMANCE ❞

Morris

In 'Entrepreneurship in established organisations: the case of the public sector', Morris and Jones argue that entrepreneurship is a universal construct that can be applied to public sector organisations:[1]

> The definition, process, nature, and underlying dimensions of entrepreneurship are fundamentally the same regardless of the context. There are, however, fundamental differences in organisational realities, suggesting that the goals, constraints, approaches, and outcomes related to successful entrepreneurial efforts are unique in public sector organisations. (p.10)

The following is an edited extract from the full text which also includes a review of entrepreneurship and public administration literature and the results of a survey of public sector managers.

[1] Morris, M.H. & Jones, F.F. (1999). 'Entrepreneurship in established organisations: the case of the public sector' in *Entrepreneurship Theory and Practice*, No.Fall, pp.71-91.

Public sector organisations are often conceptualised as monopolistic entities facing captive demand, enjoying guaranteed sources and levels of financing, and being relatively immune from the influences of voters and stakeholders.

Not only are most of the components of this stereotype inaccurate, but the contemporary public sector organisation faces unprecedented demands from a society that grows more complex and interdependent by the day. The external environment of public sector organisations can be characterised as highly turbulent, which implies an increasingly dynamic, hostile, and complex set of environmental conditions.

Available research suggests that entrepreneurship represents an effective strategic response to environmental turbulence, and there is a growing body of evidence to suggest that, under such conditions, a company's entrepreneurial orientation is positively associated with numerous measures of corporate performance.

The term 'entrepreneurship' has historically referred to the efforts of an individual who takes on the odds in translating a vision into a successful business enterprise; but, more recently, entrepreneurship has been conceptualised as a process that can occur in organisations of all sizes and types. Hence, terms like social entrepreneurship, corporate entrepreneurship and community entrepreneurship have come into vogue.

Approached more broadly, entrepreneurship refers to the process of creating value by bringing together unique cominations of resources to exploit opportunities. This process requires both an entrepreneurial event and an entrepreneurial agent. The event refers to the development and implementation of a new concept, idea, process, product, service, or venture. The agent is an individual or group who assumes personal responsibility for bringing the event to fruition.

The entrepreneurial process has both attitudinal and behavioural components. Attitudinally, it refers to the willingness of an individual or organisation to embrace new opportunities and take responsibility for effecting creative change; whilst behaviourally the process includes the set of activities required to identify, evaluate, resource and implement the concept or venture.

Underlying entrepreneurial attitudes and behaviours are three key dimensions: innovativeness, risk taking, and proactiveness. Innovativeness refers to the seeking of creative, unusual, or novel solutions to problems and needs; risk taking involves the willingness to commit significant resources to opportunities having a reasonable chance of failure; and proactiveness is concerned with implementation and usually involves considerable perseverance, adaptability and a willingness to assume responsibility for failure.

To the extent that an undertaking demonstrates some amount of innovativeness, risk taking and proactiveness, it can be considered an entrepreneurial event, and the person behind it an entrepreneur. Further, any number of entrepreneurial events can be produced in a given time period. Accordingly, entrepreneurship is not an either/or determination, but a question of degree and frequency. Organisations can be characterised, then, in terms of their entrepreneurial orientation or 'intensity', which is a reflection both of how many entrepreneurial things they are doing, and how innovative, risky, and proactive those things tend to be.

Turning to the public sector, considerable attention has been paid to the need to 'reinvent' government using market related mechanisms such as competition, market segmentation and customer focus; however, it is the argument for the development of creative, risk-taking cultures inside of public organisations which has led to the use of the term 'public sector entrepreneurship'. Its initial use in the public administration literature was focused on the visionary leader, the pursuit of social, political or economic change by individuals or groups, or as a by-product of the application of strategic management and leadership principles.

Yet, in spite of the growing attention devoted to the phenomenon, a generally accepted definition of public sector entrepreneurship

Morris

has yet to emerge. Examples of proposed definitions include the following:

> - an active approach to administrative responsibility that includes generating new sources of revenue, providing enhanced services, and helping to facilitate increased citizen education and involvement (Bellone & Goerl, 1992);[2]

> - a continuous attempt to apply resources in new ways so as to heighten the efficiency and effectiveness of public institutions (Osborne & Gaebler, 1992);[3]

> - the purposeful and organised search for innovative changes in public sector organisations and operations (Linden, 1990).[4]

Themes that emerge from these definitions include the notion that a process is involved, that entrepreneurship is ongoing, and that the end result is innovative, proactive behaviour. Building on these themes, a working definition is proposed:

> Public sector entrepreneurship is the process of creating value for citizens by bringing together unique combinations of public and/or private resources to exploit social opportunities.

There are differences, nonetheless, between public and private sector organisations that raise fundamental questions regarding not simply whether entrepreneurship can be applied in public enterprises, but whether it should be applied. Some might argue that entrepreneurship can result in innovative devices for circumventing voter approval and increasing the autonomy of public officials and public administrators, thereby undermining democracy. Further, entrepreneurship entails the pursuit of opportunity regardless of resources currently controlled, while public sector managers are limited often by legislative or regulatory statute to using only those resources formally assigned to their organisation. Finally, the mission, structure, and major initiatives of the public organisation are dictated from outside sources (legislative bodies, councils, authorities). Public managers are expected to implement these dictates in a reasonably effective and efficient manner.

[2] Bellone, C. J., & Goerl, G. F. (1992). 'Reconciling public entrepreneurship and democracy'. *Public Administration Review*, 52(2), 130-134.
[3] Osborne, D. & Gaebler, T. A. (1992). *Reinventing government: How the entrepreneurial spirit is transforming the public sector*. Reading, MA: Addison-Wesley.
[4] Linden, R. (1990). *From vision to reality: Strategies of successful innovators in government*. Charlottesville, VA.

Entrepreneurship, alternatively, represents an internal dynamic that can serve to redirect the strategic course of an organisation, potentially putting it in conflict with its stated mission or mandate. Similarly, entrepreneurial efforts can lead public enterprises to generate new services or fund-raising schemes that effectively put them in competition with private sector enterprises, which the private sector might argue is a form of unfair competition.

The counter argument is that there have always been elements of innovation and entrepreneurship in public sector organisations, and that the issue is more one of formally defining the entrepreneurial role and then determining appropriate degrees and frequencies of entrepreneurship for a given organisation or unit. Creating value for customers, putting resources together in unique ways, and being opportunity-driven are not inherently in conflict with the purpose of public agencies.

There is, one could further suggest, a growing need for entrepreneurial approaches in public administration. The contemporary environment confronting public sector managers is far more complex, threatening, and dynamic than in years past. The ability of organisations to recognise and adequately respond to their changing circumstances is severely limited not only by resources but by the management philosophies and structures that characterise public enterprises.

The question of democracy has been considered by Bellone and Goerl (1992), agreeing that potential conflicts do exist between public entrepreneurship and democracy, but suggesting that these can be bridged with what they refer to as a "civic-regarding entrepreneurship".[5] This concept emphasises accountability, in that the principles of democratic theory are incorporated into the design of any entrepreneurial initiatives.

In noting that "a strong theory of public entrepreneurship requires a strong theory of citizenship" (p. 133), they argue that such initiatives

[5] Op. cit., Bellone and Goerl

should be developed in ways that facilitate citizen education and participation. They cite, as examples of ways to accomplish such participation, citizen budget committees, advisory boards, vehicles for elevating citizen choice (e.g. vouchers) and volunteerism.

In practice, the public sector entrepreneur confronts unique obstacles. Ramamurti (1986) discusses multiplicity and ambiguity of goals, limited managerial autonomy and high political interference, high visibility, skewed reward systems, a short-term orientation (reinforced by budget and election cycles) and restrictive personnel policies.[6] To these we would add lack of competitive incentives for improved performance, difficulties in segmenting or discriminating among users, and lack of accountability among managers for innovation and change.

Approached differently, however, obstacles such as these can be used to facilitate entrepreneurial behaviour. For instance, Ramamurti (1986) proposes that goal ambiguity is a potential source of discretion to the entrepreneurial manager, that the media can be used as a source of power, and outsiders can be co-opted to enable one to take organisational risks without taking personal risks.[7]

"CREATING VALUE, PUTTING TOGETHER RESOURCES IN UNIQUE WAYS AND BEING OPPORTUNITY-DRIVEN DO NOT CONFLICT WITH THE PURPOSE OF PUBLIC AGENCIES"

To better understand the nature and role of entrepreneurship, a survey was administered to a large cross-section of South African public sector organisations. South Africa was deemed to be an especially relevant venue in which to conduct the study given the high levels of turbulence that have surrounded the transformation to democracy and a majority

---

[6] Ramamurti, R. (1986). Public entrepreneurs: Who they are and how they operate. *California Management Review*, 28(3), 142-158
[7] Ibid.

government. Moreover, the public sector is being asked to extend an array of services to sizable sections of the populace who have historically been discriminated against, and to do so while relying on a relatively limited tax base. The findings of the survey indicate that public sector managers clearly recognise entrepreneurship as a salient concept for their operations. They perceive entrepreneurship to be a key factor in promoting efficiency, improving productivity, and delivering better service to the public. Further, it is applicable at both the individual and organisational levels, but moreso at the individual level. At both levels, the traits they associate with entrepreneurship tend to reflect proactiveness and innovativeness moreso than risk taking.

It is clear that strong leadership is necessary to overcome what most respondents suggest is an environment that severely constrains entrepreneurial behaviour. Senior management must first establish goals and strategies for entrepreneurship. An important component here is the need to determine where within their organisation to place the entrepreneurial priorities. Different degrees and amounts of entrepreneurial behaviour would seem appropriate depending on the agency, department, functional area, or other organisational unit of analysis, and managerial expectations should reflect such differences.

It is also imperative that senior management perform the symbolic behaviours that reinforce the priority given to innovative thinking. Employee values and attitudes must be the focal point, especially the tendencies to resist change and to avoid failure at all costs. The facilitation of entrepreneurship ultimately comes down to people, individuals who will champion innovation and change. Mintzberg (1996, p.82), in suggesting that public sector professionals need to be freed both from the direct controls of bureaucracy and the narrow pressures of market competition, notes that "government desperately needs a life force .. there is no substitute for human dedication".[8]

[8] Mintzberg, H. (1996). Managing government, governing management. *Harvard Business Review*, 74(May-June), 75-83.

Reward and measurement systems would appear to represent especially useful tools for accomplishing some of this required attitudinal change, yet in practice they appear to serve as a leading obstacle. Training is also important. While it is debatable as to whether or not one can be taught to be an entrepreneur, public sector employees would benefit from a better appreciation for the process nature of entrepreneurship, including such issues as opportunity identification and assessment, formulation of plans for new concepts, capitalising on goal conflict and ambiguity, risk management strategies, and networking to obtain resources, among others.

There is no formal blueprint or model regarding how entrepreneurship can be accomplished in the public sector. The key appears to be experimentation. While public sector managers do not have the luxury of being able to experiment freely with structures, control systems, rewards, communication systems, or budgeting methods, there is typically more room for flex than acknowledged by so-called 'bureaucracy bashers'.

In the final analysis, we are not proposing entrepreneurship as a comprehensive framework intended to replace various models of public sector management, including models rooted in bureaucracy. However, the emergence of alternative models (e.g. the reinvention movement), as well as the findings here, suggests that conventional bureaucracy is an increasingly inadequate solution.

Our conclusion is that entrepreneurship must be an integral component in whatever models or frameworks are adopted. Entrepreneurship implies an innovative, proactive role for government in steering society towards improved quality of life. This includes generating alternative revenues, improving internal processes, and developing novel solutions to inadequately satisfied social and economic needs.

If you want to build an organization that unshackles the human spirit, you're going to need some decidedly unbureaucratic management principles.

Gary Hamel, 2006

Morris

An extract from the work of

Geoff Mulgan

Chief Executive, The Young Foundation

Positive risks: Innovation
in the public sector

"PUBLIC SECTOR INNOVATION IS ABOUT NEW IDEAS THAT WORK AT CREATING PUBLIC VALUE "

In *The Art of Public Strategy: Mobilising Power and Knowledge For the Common Good,* Mulgan considers how governments think and act, arguing that citizens benefit when governments resist the "tyranny of the immediate" by creating spaces for thought, learning and reflection:[1]

> During periods of rapid change governments have to learn quickly from their environment, relying on networks as much as hierarchies, and tapping dispersed learning as well as the assumptions of the centre…They also have to learn to learn, and to experiment, even if that sometimes means failing. The instinct of most bureaucracies is to respond to failure with more rules and tighter controls. But lasting improvements come from innovation and the discovery, or adaptation, of new knowledge. (p.3)

The following is extracted from Chapter 8 in which he considers the relationship between innovation and risk in the public sector.

---

[1] Mulgan, G. (2009). *The Art of Public Strategy: Mobilising Power and Knowledge For the Common Good*, OUP.

Charles Dickens' novel Little Dorrit describes the Circumlocution Office at the centre of the government machine which decided 'what should NOT be done'. The office reliably killed any ideas which might make government better. Dickens reflected the conventional wisdom, according to which public organisations cannot innovate. Bureaucracies lack the competitive spur that drives businesses to create new products and services. Their rules squeeze out anything creative or original. Their staff are penalised for mistakes but never rewarded for taking successful risks. So while business develops new chips, iPods, aircraft, and wonder drugs, the slow and stagnant public sector acts as a drag on everyone else.

This account is commonplace, but it's not the whole story. The public sector is not short of the combination of crisis and curiosity that so often drives new ideas. Two of the most profound innovations of the last fifty years— the Internet and the World Wide Web—came out of public organisations; and NASA must rank as one of the most successful and innovative institutions of modern times—a very rare example of a public agency using competition to achieve its ends (three competing groups of employees were tasked with designing a way to land a man on the moon—the winners came up with the very lateral idea of a spacecraft that decomposed into separate units).

Even today, the caricature of public agencies as stagnant enemies of creativity is disproven by the innovation of thousands of public servants around the world who have discovered novel ways of combating AIDS, promoting fitness, educating or vaccinating vast populations.

Yet there are good reasons to doubt the public sector's ability to innovate. Innovators usually succeed despite, not because of, dominant structures and systems. Too many good ideas are frustrated, filed away, or simply forgotten. Public services remain poor at learning from better models—even on their doorstep—and only a handful of governments have any roles, budgets, or teams devoted to innovation in their main areas of activity: welfare, security, health, or the environment. The process of planning, and sometimes of strategy, involves using existing data and concepts and applying them to new situations: creativity by contrast involves imagining new concepts and categories. Despite the rhetorical lip service paid to innovation, no government has anything remotely comparable to the armies of civil servants employed to count things, to inspect, and to monitor, or for that matter to support technological research and development (R&D).

In the public sector, as in other fields, innovation can mean many different things. It can mean new ways of organising things (like Public Private Partnerships), new ways of rewarding people (like performance-related pay), or new ways of communicating (like ministerial blogs). The simplest definition is that public sector innovation is about new ideas that work at creating public value. The ideas have to be at least in part new (rather than improvements); they have to be taken up (rather than just being good ideas); and they have to be useful. By this definition, innovation overlaps with, but is different from, creativity and entrepreneurship.

"THE MOST IMPORTANT CHARACTERISTIC OF AN INNOVATIVE FIRM IS THAT IT HAS AN EXPLICIT SYSTEM OF INNOVATION WHICH PERVADES THE WHOLE ORGANISATION"

There is a vast literature on technological and business innovation but much less on innovation in the public sector. What most of the literature confirms is that in the past public innovation has tended to be patchy, uncertain, and slow, with occasional bursts of activity. But there have been exceptions—and some cases where public service innovations evolved well ahead of the private sector.

Most people scoffed at the idea of the Open University; however, it has massively expanded participation in higher education through bringing in new students, adult, not necessarily pre-qualified, and part-time students. It has made full use of new communications technologies as they came along, from satellites to the web, and almost every part of its model has subsequently been copied by the private sector. NHS Direct is another example which succeeded by combining three existing elements in a new way: the telephone, nurses, and computers with diagnostic software. Within a few years it was receiving many millions of calls each year (2 million people use the service each month) and evaluations showed that its diagnoses were as reliable as doctors meeting patients face to face.

There are, however, some very good reasons why public sectors shouldn't innovate more. There is a lower tolerance for risk where people's lives are involved and much of the public sector is involved in far more essential services than the private sector. It can be argued that the public sector should be a stabilising force, a buffer against too much change. Ideas may rain in from ambitious politicians or hustling entrepreneurs—but bureaucrats should move slowly and take the long view.

Unfortunately these good arguments against bad innovation are often joined by much weaker arguments, as well as being amplified by structural features of the public sector which guarantee that too few good ideas make the transition from imagination to reality:

No one's job: vast bureaucracies oversee regulation but few government departments have a board member responsible for innovation.

Risk aversion: more weight is applied to discouraging risk-taking than to rewarding it; and the media gives as much weight to a small failure as to a big one.

Too many rules: innovation is squeezed out by the rules which are designed to stop capricious and unpredictable actions; and people attracted to working in big bureaucracies tend to be less creative and less at home with risk.

Uncertain results: the dilemma of introducing new innovations which will not, in the first instance, be as effective as existing practices (cars were once less reliable than horses).

Six elements of an innovative public sector

So, innovation happens—but it happens as much by chance as by design, and public innovators are usually marginalised. What can be done to put this right? There can be no simple formula for making governments creative or innovative but there are likely to be common elements.

Leadership and Culture

Political and official leaders should establish a culture in which innovation is seen as natural. There is evidence to suggest that innovative organisations become more innovative over time suggesting that innovative cultures can be self-reinforcing.[2]

Pushes and Pulls

Pushes may come from a political leadership that feels a need for new ideas (e.g. a crisis, financial necessity) or from new technology. Pulls come from the recognition of a need that isn't being met such as care, jobs or housing. The best public innovators are good at empathy and good at listening to what it is that people really want or need. Michael Young, who conceived of both the OU and NHS Direct, got many of his best ideas from random conversations on street corners and on buses.

Creativity and Recombination

It is important to see things in new ways and to learn from the people most immersed in a problem—look at how people are themselves solving their problems and start from the presumption that they are 'competent interpreters' of their own lives.[3] As Linus Pauling (who won Nobel prizes in chemistry and peace) observed, 'the best way to get good ideas it to have lots of ideas and throw the bad ones away'.

Prototypes and Pilots

Anything genuinely innovative is almost certain not to go quite according to plan. It's vital to have some measure of success, but judgement and experience count for as much as the numbers: people who have seen the trials and tribulations of past innovations are much better placed to make judgements than

---

[2] Robert L. Savage, 'Policy Innovativeness as a Trait of American States,' *Journal of Politics*, 40 (1978), 212-24.
[3] This was Richard Sennett's characterisation of Michael Young's method—in *Porcupines in Winter* (London: Young Foundation, 2006).

generalist officials or ministers: As Rosabeth Moss Kanter put it, every success looks like a failure in the middle.[4] A classic example of the pitfalls of evaluation is the experience of the High/Scope Perry pre-school programme and similar programmes launched in the USA in the 1960s. For ten years or so, the evaluations of these programmes were generally negative. It was only later that it became clear that they could achieve impressive paybacks in terms of better education and lower crime.

Scaling and Diffusion

There isn't enough political capital around to impose many new ideas. When diffusion does happen successfully, it's often because of effective champions; because of strong networks (including within the professions); plenty of hand-holding; and last but not least some financial inducements.

Sophisticated risk management

Any programme of innovation has to be smart about risks and how they should be managed. Generally it will be easier to take risks when there's a consensus that things aren't working. It will be easier if public sectors are honest about experimenting with a range of options, rather than pretending that all will succeed. It will be easier where users have some choice—e.g. of school or doctor—rather than having a new model forced upon them.

Organising for innovation

If these are some of the likely elements of an innovative system how should they be pulled together? John Kao has written that the most important characteristic of an innovative firm is that it has an explicit system of innovation which pervades the whole organisation, which is visible, known about, generates a stream of new ideas, and is seen as vital to creating new value.[5]

---

[4] Rosabeth Moss Kanter, *Rosabeth Moss Kanter on the Frontiers of Management* (Boston: Harvard Business School, 1997).

[5] J. Kao, Jamming: *The Art and Discipline of Corporate Creativity* (New York: Harper Business, 1996).

No public agencies have anything quite comparable. But such a system is what many governments need, working with the other organisations that contribute most directly to collective intelligence, including universities, business and NGOs. Doing this requires that they balance innovation-friendly internal structures, processes, and cultures with sufficient porousness and permeability to make the most of innovations that come from outside. In other words, public sectors need to exercise their own 'innovation muscles' and cultivate their hinterlands. Doing that requires that internal institutions of governance regularly assure that there is an adequate flow of potential new ideas, ranging from high risk and high impact to ones which are relatively low risk but also likely to be low in impact. It requires that there are teams and networks dedicated to organising innovation.

These need to include people to scan the world and other sectors for promising ideas (and in some cases governments may be wise to prioritise effective following rather than original innovation—what Paul Geroski and Markides Constantinos called the 'fast second' strategy).[6] They need people to map current pilots and pathfinders and assess which ones are worth building up; and to design new innovations, incubate them, and then launch them.

Experience suggests that these teams generally work best with a mix of skills, experience, and contacts, combining civil servants, social entrepreneurs, designers, and practitioners. That may be easiest to organise at arm's length through units combining 'insiderness' and 'outsiderness' or through 'skunk works'.[7] Some people need to be explicitly employed to act as brokers and intermediaries—making links between emerging ideas and changing needs. These brokers can play a vital role in protecting innovators outside the state who are bound to be attacked by threatened vested interests.

[6] Constantinos C. Markides and Paul A. Geroski, *Fast Second: How Companies Bypass Radical Innovation to Enter and Dominate New Markets* (San Francisco: Jossey Bass, 2005).
[7] 'Skunk works' refers to a semi-independent group set up to innovate within an organisation and which is less restricted by bureaucracy.

71

Teams for innovation are bound to benefit from including people who have proven track records of public innovation, but such people are often prickly, ill-suited to conventional careers and management structures. So alongside recruitment and development policies that don't squeeze out creative people, and training courses that acclimatise officials to innovative processes, pay arrangements also need to be designed to encourage risk taking (for example with bonuses when ideas are taken up).

Public sectors are often poor at innovation from within, and poor at learning from outside. They contain many innovative people but aren't good at harnessing their talents and imagination. They too rarely cultivate a plurality of alternatives and too often impose ill conceived innovations on whole regions or countries.

Innovation is an integral part of being strategic—recognising that all strategies need to create new knowledge as well as using existing knowledge. It's also a tool for helping public organisations return to the underlying motivations of public service, which should be not only about doing good, but also about always striving to do better.

Despite the rhetorical lip service paid to innovation, no government has anything remotely comparable to the armies of civil servants employed to count things...

Geoff Mulgan 2009

Mulgan

on inspiration

the entrepreneurial organisation

An interview with

Julian Birkinshaw

Professor of Strategic and International Management,
London Business School

Empowering the frontline

“ PUBLIC SECTOR MANAGERS NEED TO TAKE CALCULATED RISKS TO DRIVE THEIR ORGANISATIONS INTO THE FUTURE ”

Birkinshaw

The definition of entrepreneurship favoured by Professor Julian Birkinshaw describes entrepreneurs as individuals who pursue opportunities without regard to the resources they control. "Entrepreneurs", he says, "do not allow themselves to be confined by their formal position or their authority to get things done. They are prepared to get into alliances with others and are prepared to persuade stakeholders to change their views in order to bend them to their will".

Birkinshaw views entrepreneurship as a sub-set of leadership: "It is a much more specific definition of what people do; for example, corralling resources to satisfy a latent or clear opportunity". Leadership, on the other hand, is more broadly defined as a process of social influence by which people are persuaded to a point-of-view by virtue of a leader's vision or charisma. In many cases, entrepreneurs and leaders are one and the same: "The entrepreneur exercises leadership in pursuit of opportunities".

The challenges of managing private and public sector companies are largely similar, but Birkinshaw distinguishes the public from the private sector by its diverse set of stakeholders all with legitimate claims to influence. Notwithstanding, he says it is vital that the public sector requires of its executives strong leadership concerning the direction of their organisations: "There are too many public sector leaders who do not take a strong enough position in terms of the potential future of their organisation".

Leadership articulates a vision that people want to follow and it's imperative that public sector organisations have good leaders. It is equally important, however, that they have good managers - people who get stuff done. In *Reinventing Management*, he makes the case for 'getting stuff done'; arguing for a shift of emphasis from strategy and leadership to managerial graft: "...the aggrandisement of leadership at the expense of management is unhelpful, because management – as a profession and as a concept – is vitally important to the business world".[1] Leadership and management, though, are complementary and not at odds. Public sector managers need all

the qualities of good leadership but they also they need to be very good at following through on their ideas.

He fears, though, that irrespective of the management model employed, the tendency in these turbulent cost-cutting times will be to pull control back to the centre and says that this will be absolutely the wrong thing to do. The current climate will create new opportunities and generate new ideas and the need for flexibility and responsiveness will be crucial.

Centralisation, under these circumstances, is born of risk avoidance and Birkinshaw believes that risk avoidance is, of itself, a risk-inducing strategy. Decisions need to be made where the knowledge and the expertise is; what Birkinshaw refers to as 'high quality insight': "Organisations must build systems that put the right information in the hands of those making risk management decisions, and transfer that information into insight through deep experience".[2] If government isn't prepared to devolve power to the front line and a Chief Executive

---

[1] Birkinshaw, J.M. 2010. *Reinventing management: Smarter choices for getting things done.* Jossey-Bass. p.14
[2] Birkinshaw, J.M. and Jenkins, H. 2009. 'Risk management get personal: Lessons from the credit crisis'. AIM Research Executive Briefing. p.6

isn't prepared to push his or her organisation towards where the opportunities are, then that organisation becomes irrelevant and loses its way and that is also a risk.

Personal accountability has an important role in risk management. Every public sector Chief Executive knows that he or she is accountable in a highly visible way; but Birkinshaw believes that empowerment and accountability have a place several levels below the Chief Executive. The Chief Executive should rightfully own all of the risk but they are often in entirely the wrong place to make an effective risk assessment. Organisations, private or public, need to ensure that those closest to the riskier decisions are empowered to make those decisions and are held responsible for that empowerment.

This, he says, is the nature of hierarchy: putting the right people in the right place and holding them responsible for making the smartest choices. The Chief Executive is then in a position to own the risk – be

accountable for the decisions of his or her managers - safe in the knowledge that they will make the choices that the Chief Executive would make if he or she had that information to hand.

For risk-management by personal accountability to work, Birkinshaw says that a supportive culture is essential. The onus is on the Chief Executive to ensure that all employees empowered to make decisions receive consistent and transparent messages and understand exactly the repercussions of their actions. He believes that employee empowerment and accountability has failed – spectacularly in the case of the financial sector - because the process has been dehumanised.

Accountability tends to be less about an employee understanding the consquences of his or her actions – the bigger picture – and more about them following a process. Organisations need formal systems to function but they also thrive on the right people in the right places making the right decisions. Whilst effective risk-management is hampered

Birkinshaw

by too many decision makers, it is also hampered by the wrong decision makers. Asking the Chief Executive to sign off on everything, he stipulates, is not effective risk-management.

The establishment of 'boundaries' is essential for any organisation, giving those empowered to act appropriate limits to their freedom to act. Birkinshaw identifies three categories of boundary which safe-guard employees, customers, the public and the public purse.

Mission critical boundaries relate to safety and legal issues and assure the protection of the people who work for and come into contact with the organisation. These are non-negotiable boundaries and, if breached, must result in dismissal. Moral and ethical boundaries establish parameters for the right ways of behaving when working for and in an institution (in the education sector these would include teaching pratices, plagiarism, etc.).

Then there is what Birkinshaw

"ASKING THE CHIEF EXECUTIVE TO SIGN OFF ON EVERYTHING IS NOT EFFECTIVE RISK-MANAGEMENT"

refers to as the 'grey zone': this covers less tangible issues such as those relating to the safe-guarding of public money. This, he says, is "the tricky one" and it is the most challenging one for the aspiring entrepreneurial Chief Executive in the public sector. There can be "terrible errors of judgment" such as gambling with public money on the stock market; but, there is also the more subtle error of not taking calculated risks; in the case of colleges, for example, building new courses and new offerings to students, seeking out new types of student, seeking new ways of delivering to students and investing in new technologies.

It is Birkinshaw's contention that we have failed in our duty to invest the public's money wisely if we identify but fail to act upon an opportunity that is likely to deliver increased value for our stakeholders. It is referred to as 'false negative' in risk assessment - failing to act on opportunities that materialise - and is difficult to identify and quantify for the purposes of performance assessment. A 'false positive' – investing in opportunities that fail to materialise – is, on the other hand, highly visible. Birkinshaw believes that this has led to too many public sector managers, knowing that one type of risk is so potentially grievous they are likely to lose their jobs over it, choosing errors of omission over errors of commission. It is better for their career in the short-term to avoid the 'opportunities' that may be better for their stakeholders in the long-term.

Birkinshaw is clear that public sector managers need to take calculated risks to drive their organisations into the future; but he is equally clear that colleges must prepare their students for that future. They should deliver an education designed not only to promote excellence in the practice of their trade or profession but also to prepare them to survive in a rapidly developing freelance economy: "Do not just prepare them for a lifetime of being employed by somebody else. Given them the skills they need to go it alone or work in a smaller organisation".

He acknowledges that teaching some of the more behavioural aspects of entrepreneurship are difficult but he is absolutely certain of the importance of trying: "Give people the basics of what business is about; of running and financing a business; of incorporating a business; of finding business partners; of writing a business plan – these are all critical things".

The London Business School uses successful entrepreneurs as teaching adjuncts. This, he says, is not just a question of methodology; it's also a question of supply and demand. The sector is in the early stages of introducing entrepreneurship education alongside business and vocational education and training and there are simply not enough academics to go round; but, he adds, "some of the School's most popular courses are those led by active entrepreneurs".

Birkinshaw

An interview with

Caroline Casey

Social Entrepreneur, Founder of Kanchi

The business of social change

" EMPLOYEES NEED TO TAKE RISKS IF YOU WANT THEM TO BRING IN NEW IDEAS "

Casey

When Caroline Casey was first described as an entrepreneur, everything fell into place. "My God", she said, "that's what I am!". She wasn't some kind of misfit. Those quirky characteristics had a name and it was OK to be the kind of person she was and to work in the way that she wanted to work. Until then, all she knew was that she had identified a social problem and was working towards a solution; but now she knew she was a social entrepreneur and part of a community of entrepreneurs.

The problem she had identified was the negative mindset around disability – the fact that nobody talked about the abilities of people with disabilities and the value that they could bring to the social and business world; and her solution was Kanchi, an organisation dedicated to working with leaders in business, government and the media to encourage employers to become champions of ability, valuing the talent and ability of people with disabilities.

Entrepreneurs, she says, are visionary, creative and relentless. They're great starters and great energisers and they get things off the ground. They believe in and act upon their own intuition, and they make things happen. There is also, she says, a 'dark' side: "Entrepreneurship is deeply personal. We need to prove ourselves, we need recognition and we need to show that "we can". If you scratch the surface of any entrepreneur, you will see that something happened somewhere in their past – particularly with social entrepreneurs – and they are motivated by a very personal issue."

It is nature, she says, and not nurture. You can enhance people's working lives by imparting entrepreneurial skills and encouraging entrepreneurial behaviour, but you can't instill that energy. It's primal. It's there or it isn't. And this, she says, is a good thing: "If we were all entrepreneurs, or could all become entrepreneurs, there would be no managers; and the world needs managers because entrepreneurs are not great on process. They see what's possible but they don't see what's impossible. They can start something but they can't always make it work."

This is what she calls the "conundrum of the founder". People buy into the founder - buy into their vision, their ability to communicate their vision and into the business that will deliver it. But that is just the beginning and the business needs to succeed and the only true asset, at that early stage, is the personality and work ethic of the founder.

So, Casey started to identify mentors who could advise her on how to take Kanchi forward. It was not easy for them or for me, she says, but she needed somebody to tell her what she wasn't very good at. She had created the business – she was good at that – but what she was not good at was the management stuff such as processes, efficiencies and Board interaction.

Finding a manager to complement an entrepreneur is never easy: "Having gone through this three times now", she says, "I can tell you that it is an exceptionally difficult thing to do; but getting it right stands between the success and failure of a social enterprise." You need, she says, a process person, but the organisation you have created is young and energetic and innovative and that person cannot be completely risk averse.

You need to find a "fit of culture" so that their processes, procedures and efficiencies will protect the business whilst allowing people to take the risks that are inherent in a creative environment. The sooner in the life-cycle of the entrepreneur that you can convince them they need to let go and let somebody else in, she says, the better for the business: "It is important. Really important. Most entrepreneurs are workaholics. We just are and it's not sustainable."

Risk is a by-product of creativity and that, for Casey, makes failure inevitable: "It's the nature of innovation. Some things will work and some things will not work and it's how you handle the failure. It's horrible to fail – horrible. But it's how you handle the failure and how you approach the possibility of failure within the organisation. Employees need to take risks if you want them to bring in new ideas; and if they are afraid of failure they will not be "utterly and completely creative."

This is not, she says, detrimental to the end-user of the social enterprise: "There are many people doing what I'm doing for people with disabilities and, together, we will find a solution; but we need to do things differently or nothing will change. My value-add is that I'm taking a risk. I can only make things better. I can only add to the field. The only person who can lose is me - my ego - my reputation." In this light, Casey doesn't accept that loss is always failure: "We recently invested €100K and we didn't win; but we gained experience and we communicated what we learned. It was an investment in learning and that helped us to win the next time."

Casey is uncompromising about the overriding importance of all employees in the success of a business: "I will tell you flat out that my team and my sponsors are more important than anything or anybody – more important even than the people we serve – because if you have a dysfunctional team you are not going to be serving anybody. You're just not. You need a healthy team. I don't care how visionary you are and I don't care how innovative or dynamic you are. If your team is broken, there's no way they're going to be able to do the job."

Casey

Her organisation is in the business of social change and it aims to be a very successful business, but it's all about its people: "The critical thing is how emotionally aware – how emotionally intelligent – the managers are; because if you are emotionally intelligent, you can train and empower anyone to be successful and add value to the organisation."

She recently stepped down from the role of CEO but first ensured she had instilled a culture that was intrinsically Kanchi: "It doesn't matter who comes in and out of this company. When they come in they are a Kanchi person doing things the Kanchi way. It's the only way to perpetuate everything that has made Kanchi the company it is today – a company that is about positive reinforcement, respect for diversity, difference, dynamism and vision – a really high energy organisation."

While Casey is convinced that you cannot make somebody an entrepreneur, she strongly believes in the provision of a learning environment that can help the latent entrepreneur to discover and understand their entrepreneurial nature and gain the basic skills they need to help them along their way. You need, she says, to find a way to "flip the switch" - to turn a light on in somebody's head and let them believe.

Coaching and mentoring are important but role models are more important – role models at all levels of entrepreneurship – small, large, not-for-profit organisations – not just the Bill Gateses and the Richard Bransons. The more role models, she says, the greater the chance of a student meeting someone they can relate to: "It really works. Entrepreneurs' stories – not just one story but all the stories – are hugely beneficial in switching on those lights. The trials and tribulations and the ups and downs; stories are a fabulous way of helping to articulate what we entrepreneurs are."

She feels very strongly about personal self-awareness; that people need to know who they are as individuals, why they operate the way they do, and that they are more than they ever imagined themselves to be. Bring the entrepreneurs into the classroom, she says. Ask us to speak about anything and we will.

Why? Because we've all been there.

It is very rare, she says, for an entrepreneur to turn down an opportunity to visit and encourage an entrepreneurial group: "We have great pride in our identity - a real pride in being an entrepreneur. Entrepreneurship is about creation. It creates jobs. It creates things. It creates solutions. We know that in this time of recession, we need people to get out there and start a small business or improve an existing one and be entrepreneurial. Why? Because it's about creating employment and it's about creating solutions."

The really critical thing, she says, is getting people to ask the right questions, and one of the right questions is "why can't I?". And, importantly to Casey, once people have asked that question she wants them to understand the possibility and importance of running a social enterprise: "There's so much happening. Our sector is so exciting. We work professionally, to the highest standards. We don't cut corners and we never play the 'worthy' card. We're a business."

The one thing, she says, that entrepreneurs are not good at is asking for help; and the one thing they absolutely need is help. They need to know that they need the right people around them; they need to know where the money is; they need to know where to find the resources to write a business plan. "I never had a business plan", she says. "I wish that I had. It would have been so much easier. But I'm an entrepreneur and I chased perfection and I got here anyway."

"THE MORE ROLE MODELS, THE GREATER THE CHANCE OF A STUDENT MEETING SOMEONE THEY CAN RELATE TO... IT REALLY WORKS"

Casey

An interview with

Martin Doel, OBE

Chief Executive, Association of Colleges

An entrepreneurial culture

"THE WORLD CAN CHANGE IN FIVE MINUTES AND AN ENTREPRENEURIAL ORGANISATION WILL ADAPT"

We find ourselves in times which offer an unparalleled opportunity for public sector managers to find new ways of creating additional value for their organisations: "Very occasionally", says Doel, "the tectonic plates move and, when they do, those who are quick to spot opportunities, and agile enough to take advantage of them, can transform their organisations and their prospects".

There are managers, he says, who will respond to uncertainty by waiting for a situation to resolve and a new direction to become apparent; and there are those who will be prepared to take a considered risk and be in the vanguard of setting the agenda for the transformation of public sector management. These managers will not merely be comfortable with uncertainty—they will relish the challenge of the new.

Doel is unsympathetic towards the rationale for inertia in public sector management. He does not accept the well-worn argument that public managers are justified in failing to take the initiative because of the personal consequences of public failure. There are always consequences for failure, he says, in both the private and public sectors. Public sector managers sometimes use it as an excuse to avoid tough decisions.

Whether in the private or public sector, though, you need to 'push the envelope'; not just for the sake of pushing it but with a clear view to what you are seeking to achieve. It is the job of a leader to create value for his or her stakeholders and it is the duty of a leader to keep pushing at the boundaries that prevent them from doing it.

He is similarly reluctant to accept the easy distinction that is made—often for the convenience of leadership theorists—between 'leaders' and 'managers'; contending that transformational leadership requires the competencies that are inherent in both leadership styles.

A former Air Commodore, Doel was responsible for training and development across the Armed Forces. He favours the word 'command' to describe his style of leadership; a word that jars in a civilian context but one that he uses to represent the interdependence of leadership and management: "You can't get people to come with you", he says, "if you don't know where you're going; but neither can you

get them there without the proficient management of resources".

Doel locates entrepreneurial behaviour less in the character of the leader and more in the response of leaders and subordinates to unexpected or adverse circumstances. The leader, he says, is entrepreneurial when he or she empowers subordinates to act without detailed direction; and the subordinate is entrepreneurial in exercising that freedom to deliver an objective whether or not they have immediate access to the advice or support of the leader.

This degree of delegation —of devolved decision making— requires the development of a culture within an organisation that imbues all decision makers with a comprehensive understanding of the themes and values of the organisation. In the case of the Association of Colleges, Doel has sought to instill an understanding that it is a membership facing organisation which exists to serve and promote the interests of its members. His staff are empowered to make decisions in the knowledge that every decision must be in line with the overarching goals of the organisation.

In a military context, says Doel, this is leading by 'mission-type' orders as opposed to 'detailed' orders; a style which he characterises as managing people with 'the minimum of the how and the maximum of the why'. Doel's strategy is to communicate what is required and why it needs to be done; but he aims to give his staff minimal direction on how it should be done, empowering them to use their own skills which are closer and likely to be more relevant to the task in hand.

More crucial than that, though, is the readiness of the organisation to react to change. The world, he says, can change in five minutes; but an entrepreneurial organisation will adapt because its employees have absolute clarity on both the immediate objective and the long term goals of the organisation. This, for Doel, is the essence of entrepreneurial leadership and of an entrepreneurial organisation. "Life", he says, "just never turns out the way you expect it to". It is incumbent upon the CEO to protect his or her stakeholders from the vicissitudes of fortune because the leader can't always be in the right place at the right time to do that.

It is also, he says, incumbent upon the CEO to ensure that they've put the right person in the right place to take this responsibility and to ensure that they've created an environment which protects against and deals appropriately with failure. "The critical task of the leader", says Doel, "is to create a permissive environment for people within which they can fail but in such a way that their failure is not catastrophic to the individual or the organisation". If you have identified an individual as ready for that extra responsibility, you have to protect the organisation but you also have to protect the individual: "You create a risk framework within which they have room to innovate consistent with their ability; but that framework should also enable them to learn from their experience and not be personally devastated by failure".

"YOU CAN'T GET PEOPLE TO COME WITH YOU IF YOU DON'T KNOW WHERE YOU'RE GOING"

93

Doel has noticed that under those circumstances members of staff are willing to 'have a go'—to defer full understanding of the commitment they are making because they know that information will be forthcoming and they know the risk of failure has been minimised both as a possibility and in terms of its consequences. Conversely, he has experienced, in other organisations, a tangible sense of fear where staff are given precise and detailed instructions on how to achieve a goal and very little context or understanding of the goal itself.

Doel is convinced that Colleges of Further Education are better suited to this entrepreneurial style of leadership than other educational institutions. Schools are small enough and sufficiently circumscribed to operate under direct leadership; whilst universities are unwieldy with quasi autonomous departments which render the model unworkable. FE, however, is a suitable candidate for the model both in scale and in the particular skills and attributes of its tutors.

FE principals, he says, exist on a continuum in terms of their leadership style and abilities; but he believes that the sector already has many principals who are sufficiently skilled and confident in the exercise of entrepreneurial leadership. Doel is, once again, at odds with received wisdom when he discusses the attributes of principals who will thrive in this brave new world. He does not accept that public sector managers need private sector experience.

While, he says, a broader background might seem to be an advantage, he cautions against making precipitous judgments against a candidate with a curriculum-only background: "If you've always worked in a college and benefited from working under leaders who have rewarded you for innovation and initiative; and if you've added that to your life experience, your personality and your upbringing; then you are more inclined to be the type of person who's going to take advantage of the opportunity to be an innovative and entrepreneurial leader". Commercial experience, he says, can simply be about attention to the bottom line and delivering safe profit rather than taking calculated risks to maximise value.

"I am reticent about the potential to teach leadership in a direct way", says Doel. "There are a few absolutely natural leaders and there are leaders that have little inclination or facility for leadership. The majority lie somewhere between these two poles". You can teach the knowledge-based stuff; you can talk about leadership and styles of leadership; you can discuss managerial characteristics; and you can consider what constitutes a calculated risk rather than a 'hit and hope'. This, he believes, applies in different ways to both professional leadership courses and to teaching vocational students.

He does, though, believe that there are professionals and students who have leadership qualities that lay dormant and who would benefit from exposure to inspirational entrepreneurs and from participation in experiential classrooms, workshops and, for students, commercial placements. For Doel, simulation and role-playing exercises are the most important part of any successful leadership course; exercises that are fun and confidence-building and involve reflection and feedback. He cites the BBC's

The Apprentice as a good example of a teaching model which uses experiential exercises followed by reflection and advice, albeit in a confrontational way that does not suit most learners.

For students, he says, a safe place to experience and to reflect should be at the core of any entrepreneurship programme. They need the business basics; they need to understand that they can have control over their own lives; and they need to know how to present themselves in interviews. There is a significant overlap with the creation of an entrepreneurial organisation: the provision of a safe place to fail together with encouragement, reflection, feedback and confidence-building. Not 'soft' confidence-building but a process of review and reflection which is sufficiently challenging to leave the student more self-aware and more motivated. "It just needs to be fun. Any course about entrepreneurial skills is about having a positive outlook on life and a positive approach to what you're doing; a feeling that it's fun and that we can achieve good things together and we're going to".

New wealth is created by new ideas. New ideas tend to come from new voices. Are you listening to those voices in your organisation?

Gary Hamel, 1999

the further education sector

An interview with

Dame Jackie Fisher

Chief Executive, Newcastle College Group

Making the right difference

" STEWARDSHIP IS THE BACKGROUND AGAINST WHICH I AM ENTREPRENEURIAL "

Fisher

The concept of stewardship is rarely discussed in contemporary management theory and, when it is, it is employed as a counterpoint to leadership theory, representing a practice or tendency that must be suppressed if an organisation is to thrive.

Jackie Fisher doesn't see it this way. To her, stewardship is fundamental to public sector management. She believes it should be "in the bones" of the public sector manager - an underlying ethos – a check that facilitates the balance between commercial activities and public service. Without this balance, she says, you could go "very, very badly wrong".

Fisher is a great believer in leadership but argues that stewardship *is* leadership: "If you you think it isn't", she says, "you are quite mistaken". She doesn't see stewardship merely as a trait of the leader. It should, she says, be embedded in the culture, values and operating processes of the organisation. While you can be commercially driven, have the appetite and attitudes of a private sector manager and grow your business to make as much money as you can for reinvestment, you are deploying public assets and that requires a moral compass: "Many of our values are private sector values and our operating processes are private sector processes; but that is absolutely and emphatically against the background of stewardship of the organisation, of its assets and of public funds."

Fisher's leadership style has changed throughout her career to meet different management challenges. In her current position, leading an organisation which operates out of multiple locations through a divisional structure, she has had to adopt a style of leadership which reflects the fact that she cannot know everyone or directly influence all decision makers.

Her visceral understanding of stewardship is, she believes, a result of public sector experience alone and she is convinced that it is an attribute that cannot easily be acquired from the private sector: "I have worked at a number of levels in the public sector and been taught the importance of stewarding and how to steward. I don't believe it

is something you can learn very easily if you transfer in from the private sector at the highest level."

At the core of her approach to public sector management is a sense of obligation: "If you take public money, it comes with obligations. If you recruit a 16-year old from school, there are obligations. If you let a member of the public on to your premises, there are obligations." Nonetheless, she is comfortable with describing herself as entrepreneurial and believes that most people would agree; adding that if Newcastle College is not the most entrepreneurial college in the country, it certainly is one of them.

"Are we morally-based and are we commercial and entrepreneurial?", she asks. "Yes we are. They are not mutually exclusive." She sees no tension between being a steward and being entrepreneurial: "I am stewarding the assets of the organisation and I am stewarding the deployment of and accountability for public money within the organisation. That is the background against which I am entrepreneurial."

Fisher employs 4,000 people including 300 managers, with

Fisher

over 10,000 full-time students and a total enrollment of 70,000 each year. She has acquired a large private training company, manages significant long-term government contracts and around £35 million in short-term contracts. The magnitude of the enterprise necessitates not just entrepreneurial leadership but a fully realised entrepreneurial organisation.

You couldn't, she says, run this for a single day without devolving responsibility and accountability into the organisation. It requires establishing feedback loops to give comfort that the decisions being made are the best decisions that can be made at that moment in time by the person making them: "Does that mean that we always make the right decisions? No. Do we make more right decisions than not? Yes."

People who work in colleges, says Fisher, are inherently entrepreneurial. She has created a culture, through embedding key processes, that gives people permission "to do the things they would like to do". They want to do interesting stuff, she says, and they want to push boundaries. They want to take risks but they also want guidance and support. Her experience with the private training company has informed the recruitment of new managers into the college: "It is natural to appoint people into the private company who are commercially driven and who want to get things done. We also appoint very similar people into the colleges."

Fisher has created a culture which allows people to realise their ambitions. It is a dynamic process – something, she says, which they rehearse a lot – and it is about creating ambitious and entrepreneurial managers. What you end up with, she says, are very different managers with very different appetites for and attitudes towards risk. You need to moderate some and encourage others, and you need to put

"WE'RE NOT JUST HERE TO DELIVER QUALIFICATIONS. WE'RE HERE TO MAKE A DIFFERENCE TO PEOPLE"

controls in place to ensure that no one person is in a position to cause significant damage to the long-term financial health of the organisation.

Although wholly invested in the concept of stewardship, risk management, she says, is a commercial process. It is not something she does wearing her 'steward' hat. She identifies three types of risk: routine (child protection, health and safety), operational (funding targets) and strategic (major projects). "It's a standard business model", she says. "We have processes in place at a strategic level and embedded in the running of the operation to manage those risks and to keep them under review. In addition, the Governors, on every major area of risk, set a risk appetite that they are broadly comfortable with."

Fisher doesn't use core values to evaluate risk, but she does have boundaries that she will not cross: "We would not prejudice the long-term financial health of the organisation. We would not put our students or our staff at risk." She cites an example of not progressing an overseas opportunity for revenue because she had reservations about

staff safety. We have, she says, a considered process around what we will and what we will not do: "We will not make money for the sake of it. We will only deliver that which is purposeful and meaningful."

Fisher is a realist. She recognises that sometimes you have to sit tight and await the outcome of changes in the political and funding environment: "As a public sector organisation, we are being procured to do something; therefore, sitting and waiting is an inevitability of a new Government coming in. So, am I sitting and waiting? Yes. Does that make me feel disempowered? No, not at all. It makes me think that even if all the changes are not ones we would have chosen, we need to make the best of them and I'm sure we will, and we need to make more of them than anyone else does."

She frames her response to policy implementation and change in terms of influence. The policy environment is not of her creation but it is absolutely her responsibility to influence it and to optimise her organisation's position, all the while continuing to deliver learning and qualifications and employment opportunities to as many people as possible by spreading the funding she receives as thinly as possible.

While prepared to agitate and influence from within, she would like central Government to afford her the licence that she affords her managers: "A reduction in bureaucracy would be a win – I've been waiting most of my working life for that – and a reduction in non-constructive interventions from funding bodies would also be a win."

Greater fiscal and managerial freedom, however, would not diminish the public service ethic: "Nobody would think that the only thing you could pay attention to in running an organisation like this is being commercial. It would be ludicrous. You have to be commercial and you have to have best business practice. It doesn't take away your obligations. We are a very moral organisation."

What drives her employees, says Fisher, is their desire to make a difference. Success can be reconfiguring the budget to deliver services to an additional 2,500 adults who are struggling

in a time of recession: "Because public funding has declined for adults in learning, we're getting demand now that we don't have the funding to meet. We have people in the North East who are becoming unemployed and who are uncertain and anxious about the future. Should we try and manage our budgets to allow more of those people the opportunity to get a qualification next year? The answer is yes. We're not just here to deliver qualifications. We're here to make a difference to people."

This, she says, is what motivates people who work in colleges. And this is why they are commercial— not to be profligate but to have the skills and resources to spend money wisely so that more people can benefit from their services.

Fisher

An interview with

Geoff Russell

Chief Executive, Skills Funding Agency

Entrepreneurs will make further education fit for the future

"FE COLLEGES ARE SOCIAL BUSINESSES IN THEIR OWN RIGHT"

Russell

The most successful leaders in the further education sector are those who are ambitious for their colleges, innovative in their thinking and have a strong desire to extend their abilities to other institutions.

"Further education colleges", says Russell, "are not like schools or universities. They are social businesses in their own right and do not differ greatly from private sector companies. They are run by some of the best public education business managers in the country." He expects to see successful colleges become even

more commercial and independent in the decade ahead; believing that federations, mergers or other forms of collaboration will not only be the route to survival for some colleges, but an imperative for a better FE offer fit for a tougher world.

Russell stresses the importance of creative and entrepreneurial leadership in a time of constrained public funding. An attitude of 'battening down the hatches' or 'doing less for less' will, he argues, be a wholly insufficient response to the challenges and opportunities ahead. The Business Secretary,

Vince Cable, in his inaugural letter to the Skills Funding Agency, outlined "...the pressing need to reduce bureaucracy and deliver more efficient services at lower cost" whilst also mandating for the sector the "freedom to innovate and deliver what is actually needed by employers and learners".

Russell is clear about what this will mean for the frontline: "It marks a new approach to our relationship with colleges and training organisations, offering them greater flexibility and the freedom to innovate and be enterprising. In exchange, however, we need a funding system that will motivate them to do what the best training organisations do already—engage directly with learners, employers and local partners and deliver the outcomes they need and not just qualifications."

Much of the research into public sector management has found that success is contingent upon the willingness of the leader to lead; to be a proactive and innovative manager as opposed to being a steward of the public purse. Russell is equally clear on the respective roles of the Principal,

the Board of Corporation and the Senior Leadership Team. The Principal must embody the entrepreneurial attributes of proactiveness, innovation and risk-taking; the Board should support and challenge the Principal and monitor progress; and the Senior Leadership Team should manage, led by the Senior Vice-Principal as the public sector equivalent of Chief Operating Officer.

It is essential, he says, that leaders are given the time and the space to lead. In this respect, he questions whether some Boards of Corporation are 'fit for purpose'; able to be both guardian of the organisation and advocate of the entrepreneurial leader; and whether they are agile enough to respond to changes in the economy and to the needs of the next generation of learners and employers.

College Boards are often populated by business people; but, says Russell, many of these successful private sector entrepreneurs become uncharacteristically cautious when faced with the complexities of the stewardship of a public asset. While it is generally acknowledged that there is a significant overlap between the management strategies and practices of private and public sector companies, the issues of public accountability and consensus have, he believes, been wholly underestimated, with insufficient attention given to the selection and training of managers and governors. Public service management involves negotiating top-down directives, dealing with multiple stakeholders (including 'political masters'), accepting that political exigencies trump all other priorities and responding to various and changing measures of success. It also involves negotiating the pressure for short-term delivery and a top-down default aversion to risk.

Notwithstanding his reservations about the preparedness of leaders and governors in the sector, he remains to be convinced about the contribution that leadership programmes can make to entrepreneurial leadership and is sceptical about whether entrepreneurship can be taught at all. He instinctively believes that an entrepreneurial orientation is honed through experience rather than education and training. He recommends that aspiring leaders should be exposed to different operating environments, with an emphasis on experience being more appropriate to the development of entrepreneurial leadership skills than formal programmes.

This is corroborated by experience in the US which has seen a massive rise in entrepreneurship courses over the last 20 years (more than 6,000 courses across public and private colleges and universities). Curricula are focused on learning *for* rather than *about* entrepreneurship with an emphasis on experience and applied learning and including the crucial element of learning from one's mistakes in a supportive environment. The element of applied learning is clearly demonstrated by the prevalence of teaching adjuncts who are entrepreneurs (from 75% to 100% in the top ten colleges) and in the provision of mentoring programmes.

Russell's view of the sector is informed by his experience in diverse industries and businesses. As a relative newcomer to the sector, he sees it clearly and not with an agenda honed from bitter experience. He acknowledges that colleges, in a time of relative plenty, have been incredibly successful, exceeding virtually every target set for them. Many colleges now regard the private sector as customers and have worked with over 15,000 businesses through work-based learning.

"IT IS ESSENTIAL THAT LEADERS ARE GIVEN THE TIME AND THE SPACE TO LEAD"

This, he says, should have given companies the confidence to utilise colleges for even more of their training needs; but the sector has an image problem. It may be that over-reliance on public sector funding has prevented less enterprising colleges from adopting a more aggressive and/ or commercial approach to the training market place. There is also the issue of publicly funded work-based learning that was perceived as 'free' by employers.

These programmes will change in the new fiscal environment and

that will be a good thing. Colleges that have built alliances with private sector training organisations have demonstrated greater flexibility and range in the training they can offer; and this may be where the entrepreneurial abilities of a Principal/ Chief Executive, supported by a Board and leadership team fostering a spirit of proactiveness and innovation, will almost certainly be a critical asset in the coming decade.

The ability to build new relationships and sustain profitable partnerships is valued in boardrooms across the world and is not "inherently in conflict with the purpose of public agencies".[1] If funding is realigned to outcomes, Principals will have to build strong relationships with local businesses in order to meet placement criteria and also explore business and educational opportunities in partnership with universities, academies and schools.

A more entrepreneurial orientation is, says Russell, valuable for

---

[1] Morris, M.H., Jones, F.F. (1999). "Entrepreneurship in established organisations: the case of the public sector" in *Entrepreneurship Theory and Practice*, No.Fall, pp.71-91.

both the institution and its core stakeholder—the student. The entrepreneurial student will have the confidence and the ability to add to the value of local businesses while those businesses can add value to the lives of the students they employ.

Looking across the sector, it is largely the Principal/CEOs who have taken risks in building partnerships and acquiring businesses and it is Russell's view that their time, energy and creativity should be used to interface with the outside world while their managers get on with the business of managing. He is, however, equally insistent that whilst the leader should be the innovator, they should also champion innovation within the organisation, echoing Bernier and Hafsi who propose that while "individual heroic entrepreneurship provides the quick and major bursts required for fundamental change, systemic entrepreneurship is what ensures that these revolutionary interventions have enduring effect".[2]

Russell

---

[2] Bernier, L. & Hafsi, T. (2007). 'The Changing Nature of Public Entrepreneurship'. *Public Administration Review*, 67: 408-533.

enthu

the new entrepreneurs

An interview with

Michael Furdyk

Co-Founder and Director of Technology,
TakingITGlobal

Harnessing the power of innovation

" EMBRACING FAILURE IS PART OF THE CREATIVE AND ENTREPRENEURIAL PROCESS "

Furdyk

There is a disconnect between formal education and business education and, if it isn't addressed, latent entrepreneurs—"those who need a little push or who are slightly risk averse"—may not be switched on to their potential as innovators.

Michael Furdyk believes that the secondary curriculum in North America is testing the creativity out of students, and giving teachers less and less flexibility to address the needs of a generation who are IT-adept, naturally collaborative and passionate about global issues. It is really difficult, he says,

to reverse the damage done during this time.

He advocates involving children as young as seven or eight in a learning environment which celebrates creativity and reframes failure as a logical and even valuable consequence of trying something new: "Embracing failure is part of the creative and entrepreneurial process, but that's not what we learn in school. We learn that failure is a bad thing. So we produce young people who are hesitant to pursue their ideas, when we should be producing people who will just jump in and allow a great idea to grow and develop."

Nurturing creativity, he says, is critical: "If you don't have that creative mindset when you start business classes—if you are closed to new ideas and to your power as an innovator—then your ideas just won't be that interesting."

Furdyk was in the vanguard of recognising the creative potential of online collaboration for young entrepreneurs. Together with Jennifer Corriero, he founded TakingITGlobal, a social networking site for young people to discuss and develop their ideas and to cooperate to make the world a better place.[1] To date, it has engaged over 14 million young people from every country in the world.

The underlying premise has been expanded into a business model by Furdyk's mentor, Don Tapscott, in *Wikinomics: How Mass Collaboration Changes Everything.*[2] The book posits a future where classic business and employment models are replaced by the mass collaboration of free individual agents. The sequel, *Macrowiknomics*, extends the model to the social sector—to government, education, science and healthcare: "Just as millions have contributed to Wikipedia... there is now a historic opportunity to marshal human skill, ingenuity, and intelligence on a mass scale to reevaluate and reposition many of our [social] institutions for the coming decades and for future generations."[3]

Whether in pursuit of a private, public or social enterprise, Generation Z— the Internet generation— is shifting the working paradigm. Tapscott has directly addressed the role of the internet generation in changing the world: "Net Geners are collaborators in every part of their lives. As civic activists, they're tapping into the collaborative characteristic with aplomb. The Net Gen wants to help. They'll help companies make better products and services."[4]

Tapscott, like Furdyk, believes that conventional schooling is antithetical to this new way of

[1] www.TakingITGlobal.org
[2] Don Tapscott and Anthony D. Williams, *Wikinomics: How mass collaboration changes everything*, Portfolio, 2006
[3] Don Tapscott and Anthony D. Williams, *Macrowikinomics: Rebooting business and the world*, Portfolio, 2010
[4] Don Tapscott, *Grown up Digital: How the net generation is changing your world*, McGraw-Hill, 2009

working: "Educators should take note. The current model of pedagogy is teacher focused, one-way, one size fits all. It isolates the student in the learning process."[5] Furdyk and Corriero had already grasped this concept and developed TakingITGlobal to deliver new teaching resources for secondary students: "Our aim is to lift them beyond the classroom experience—to give them the opportunity to network and collaborate—to bounce off each other and to go deeper with their learning—to connect with their teacher in the traditional sense but also with experts in the field." When the class moves on, students are still part of TakingITGlobal, belonging to a community that stays with them for life. This gives them ongoing access to a peer network for advice and support in the development of enterprises and products and services; and, as importantly, provides an alumni network that is available to the next generation of students as role models and mentors.

Furdyk's first online venture sold for over $1 million when he was just seventeen. He then turned his attention to the social sector; but instead of taking the usual path of social entrepreneurs—identifying a problem and seeking a solution—he created a resource that would enable an infinite number of people to develop numerous solutions to countless problems.

As a student, he hadn't found it particularly easy interacting with or reaching out to people but he had recognised the value of peer groups and cliques in creative endeavour. He believes himself to be in the 30% of people who simply "do not fit into the mainstream"; but they are passionate and have great ideas and they thrive in an online world.

Interested in computers from the age of two, Furdyk 'grew up' with his industry of choice as it developed, through trial and error, from word processors through PCs to the world wide web. He favours some of the sayings of Thomas Watson, the founder of IBM, who encapsulated both the importance of risk-taking and the value of failure: "Every time

Furdyk

we've moved ahead in IBM, it was because someone was willing to take a chance, put his head on the block, and try something new" and "The way to succeed is to double your error rate."

A new and more directly entrepreneurial programme for TakingITGlobal is Sprout E-course, an online resource for aspiring social entrepreneurs that focuses on the importance of mentoring.[6] Candidates develop a project plan over a 6-week e-course and are then eligible for the Pearson Fellowships for Social Innovation, awarded to the most promising ideas. Included in each Fellowship is one-to-one mentoring from experienced social innovators.

To date, the programme has matched over one hundred project plans with mentors to guide them through the process, to provide reflective feedback, and to give them more measurable skills such as pitching and public speaking. It is critical, says Furdyk, for a young entrepreneur to be able to sell his or her idea. They also need guidance on building a team, learning how to work with other people and, ultimately, growing their organisations beyond themselves.

As TakingITGlobal started to grow beyond its founders, Furdyk and Corriero were committed to building an inclusive 'entrepreneurial' organisation; creating an environment where everyone was invited to advise and to give opinions beyond the scope of their own role. At least half of the programmes developed since its inception have originated from the ideas of people who would not have been heard in a more traditional organisational structure. Furdyk had witnessed the value of empowering people—of benefiting from the "entrepreneurial eye" of those often closest to the task— while working at Microsoft.

In order to ensure that those values

"THERE ARE VERY FEW 45 YEAR OLD PROFESSIONALS WITH MBAS WALKING INTO A VC OFFICE AND SAYING I HAVE THE NEXT BIG IDEA"

[6] www.sproutecourse.org

remain a part of TakingITGlobal, they work with WorldBlu, an organisation founded by the 21 year old Traci Fenton to establish and monitor democratic practices in the work place.[7] In describing her first day at work, Fenton nicely encapsulates the failure of traditional company structures to develop and profit from their best resource: "...my wide-eyed hopes were quickly dashed when I left work that first day feeling completely dehumanized and dejected. I quickly saw that I was not going to have a voice in the workplace. I was not going to be invited to engage or have any real decision-making power."

Furdyk is passionate about the role of information technology as a powerful resource in education and as a facilitator of entrepreneurial endeavour; but he also believes that there is a crucial role for government in fostering an entrepreneurial spirit: "Sometimes the scale of the task requires the support of government as well as the availability of local and online resources. In my case, as a young entrepreneur, there was no way for me to access support and that was to my detriment. I didn't know what to do. If I had had access to today's resources, it would have saved a lot of legal headaches and accounting fees!"

He gives the example of a government programme in Canada called Summer Company where students are paid the earning equivalent of a holiday job to start-up and run their own business. They are given up to $1,500 towards start-up costs and receive hands-on business coaching and mentoring from local community business leaders. An additional $1,500 is provided upon successful completion of the programme. For Furdyk, this demonstrates the value of government involvement in the creation of an entrepreneurial culture: it can provide funding; it 'normalises' innovation and risk-taking; it 'discovers' the latent entrepreneur; and it encourages those who need a "little push".

Notwithstanding the provision of a creative learning environment, access to mentors and government support, young entrepreneurs still have to raise

Furdyk

the capital necessary to pursue their ideas. Furdyk believes that venture capitalists and angel investors are, on the whole, not risk-averse when it comes to young entrepreneurs— and that if they are, they should think again: "There are very few 45 year old professionals with MBAs walking into a VC office and saying I have the next big idea; so, if they don't want to miss out on the next big idea—the next big opportunity for their own business—they need to take even very young people very seriously."

Tapscott is equally animated in promoting the value of listening to and supporting young entrepreneurs: "What an extraordinary period in human history this is—for the first time the next generation coming of age can teach us how to ready our world for the future. The digital tools of their childhood and youth are more powerful than what exists in much of corporate America. I believe that if we listen to them and engage with them, their culture of interaction, collaboration and enablement will drive economic and social development and prepare this shrinking planet for a more secure, fair and prosperous future."[8]

---

[8] Op. cit. *Grown up Digital.*

The current model of pedagogy is teacher focused, one-way, one size fits all. It isolates the student in the learning process.

Furdyk

Don Tapscott, 2009

An extract from the work of

Heidi Neck

Jeffry A. Timmons Professor of Entrepreneurial Studies
Babson College

*Entrepreneurship education:
Known worlds and new frontiers*

"ENTREPRENEURSHIP EDUCATION HAS MORE RELEVANCE TODAY THAN EVER BEFORE "

Neck

In 'Entrepreneurship education: Known worlds and new frontiers', Neck and Greene advance the concept of teaching entrepreneurship as a method:[1]

> The method is a way of thinking and acting, built on a set of assumptions using a portfolio of techniques to create. It goes beyond understanding, knowing, and talking and requires using, applying, and acting. At the core of the method is the ability for students to practice entrepreneurship and we introduce a portfolio of practice-based pedagogies. (p.55)

The following extract concentrates on the rationale for their approach and includes a discussion of ways of learning which provide students with skills and techniques which should better prepare them for the unpredictable world of the entrepreneur.

[1] Neck, H. M. & Greene, P. G. (2011). 'Entrepreneurship Education: Known Worlds and New Frontiers'. *Journal of Small Business Management*, pp. 55-70.

Entrepreneurship is complex, chaotic, and lacks any notion of linearity. As educators, we have the responsibility to develop the discovery, reasoning, and implementation skills of our students so they may excel in highly uncertain environments. These skills enhance the likelihood that our students will identify and capture the right opportunity at the right time for the right reason. However, this is a significant responsibility and challenge.

The current approaches to entrepreneurship education are based on a world of yesterday—a world where precedent was the foundation for future action, where history often did predict the future. Yet, entrepreneurship is about creating new opportunities and executing in uncertain and even currently unknowable environments. Entrepreneurship and entrepreneurship education have more relevance today than ever before.

For many years, it was popular to ask, "Can entrepreneurship be taught?" As educators, we always said, "yes, of course" and went on to list the myriad of reasons rehearsed in advance of such questions. Our answers might include, "it is a skill set," or "we have been doing it for years," or "it depends what you mean by entrepreneurship." In reality and upon reflection in looking at the future of entrepreneurship education, we may be willing to admit that we were wrong and willing to consider alternative explanations.

For many students of entrepreneurship, whereas their peers are pursuing careers, they are pursuing a life path. It looks different, it feels different; it is different—especially in today's global environment.

We are proposing that teaching entrepreneurship requires teaching a method. The method is teachable, learnable, but it is not predictable. The method is people dependent but not dependent on a type of person. The entrepreneurship method goes beyond understanding, knowing, and talking and demands using, applying, and acting. Most importantly the method requires practice. Entrepreneurship requires practice. Learning a method, we believe, is often more important than learning specific content. In an ever-changing world, we need to teach methods that stand the test of dramatic changes in content and context. We introduce this method in light of other current approaches to teaching entrepreneurship.

The Known Worlds of Entrepreneurship Education

We present three different approaches used to teach entrepreneurship. Some educators rely on one approach, whereas others incorporate two or even all approaches.

The Entrepreneur World

The entrepreneur is the champion in this world. On the delivery side, as teachers, we use a variety of entrepreneurial assessments, self-examinations, the "do you have the right stuff" approach. We probe for those characteristics the early research suggested were important, such as locus of control or need for achievement. Many of these are interesting and valid measures but not necessarily precise for identifying entrepreneurs.

In some sense, our students taught in this world see entrepreneurship as a box in which they either fit or do not. Their concern is that they do not have the right stuff/characteristics to be an entrepreneur. As teachers, our choices of entrepreneurial illustrations set up role models and our students often do not see a reflection of themselves.

The Process World

We refer to the process world as one of planning and prediction. The analytical approach of teaching opportunity evaluation, feasibility analysis, business planning, and financial forecasting is the cornerstone for most entrepreneurship curricula today. Perhaps the process world is so popular to teach in because we can. When most agreed that entrepreneurs did not have specific traits, we were motivated to find processes to teach.

The process world in our view is one of prediction. The problem is that entrepreneurship is neither linear nor predictable, but it is easy to teach as if it were.

Neck

The Cognition World

The cognitive approach in entrepreneurship is really only about 15 years old and, with a few exceptions, has only started to make its way into the classroom in the last five years. In this world, we are again focusing on the entrepreneur or the entrepreneurial team but in a quite different way. This newer focus on the person is in a more dynamic way that recognizes the potential for learning how to think entrepreneurially.

So, what and how do we teach in this world? We pay attention to different things, including the decision to become an entrepreneur and how to understand that decision. We investigate the entrepreneur and most certainly now include the team. We spent more time on discovery, specifically on the identification and exploitation of opportunities, and we explore what we believe to be the central question of this world: how do people think entrepreneurially.

The entrepreneur world has clearly informed us that there is no one type of entrepreneur. This means one of the challenges of the cognitive world is to avoid the trap of the entrepreneur world and therefore be able to recognize the richness of a diversity of cognitive approaches, again linked to a diversity of entrepreneurial motivations and desired outcomes or definitions of success.

New Frontiers: Entrepreneurship as a Method

Why do we support entrepreneurship as a method? Because a process implies that you will get to a specific destination. Entrepreneurship is often thought of as a process—a process of identifying an opportunity, understanding resource requirements, acquiring resources, planning, and implementing.

A process is quite predictable. Entrepreneurship is not predictable. On the other hand, a method represents a body of skills or techniques; therefore, teaching entrepreneurship as a method simply implies that we are helping students understand, develop, and practice the skills and techniques needed for productive entrepreneurship.

Figure 1 contrasts teaching entrepreneurship as a process and a method:

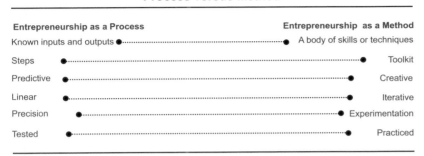

Figure 1
Process versus Method

Entrepreneurship as a Process	Entrepreneurship as a Method
Known inputs and outputs	A body of skills or techniques
Steps	Toolkit
Predictive	Creative
Linear	Iterative
Precision	Experimentation
Tested	Practiced

Teaching entrepreneurship as a method requires going beyond understanding, knowing, and talking; it requires using, applying, and acting. Entrepreneurship requires practice. Learning a method may be more important than learning content. In an ever-changing world, we need to teach methods that stand the test of dramatic changes in content and context.

Perhaps, this is ultimately the nature of entrepreneurship education. The method forces students to go beyond understanding, knowing, and talking. It requires using, applying, and acting. The method requires practice. Therefore, our underlying assumptions of the method include the following:

(1) Applies to novice and experts: the assumption is that the method applies across student populations and works regardless of experience level. What is important is that each student understands how he or she views the entrepreneurial world and his or her place in it. It represents the foundation of the method.

(2) The method is inclusive, meaning that the definition of entrepreneurship is expanded to include any organization at multiple levels of analysis. Therefore, success is idiosyncratic and multidimensional.

3) The method requires continuous practice. The focus here is on doing then learning, rather than learn then do. As a result, a reflective practice component is incredibly important to learning.

(4) The method is for an unpredictable environment. The Method approach firmly recognizes that entrepreneurship is teachable.

We suggest a portfolio here that includes starting businesses as part of coursework, serious games and simulations, design-based learning, and reflective practice.

Starting Businesses

Starting businesses as part of coursework has become more mainstream over the past few years. Babson College, for example, started its Foundations of Management and Entrepreneurship (FME) course in 1996 where first year undergraduate students are required to start a business during their first year at the college.

The overall purpose of the course is to allow students to practice business and entrepreneurship so the content comes alive. The objectives of the course include:

(1) Students practice entrepreneurship and generate economic and social value.

(2) Students understand the nature of business as an integrated enterprise and knowledge of all key business areas is essential in developing a well-rounded business aptitude in preparation for the real world.

(3) Students use information technology (IT) for decision-making and productivity and learn that IT is essential in supporting all areas of a business.

(4) Students experience social responsibility and philanthropy through the donation of their time (six hours minimum) and business profits to charitable organizations.

We are advocating for real world venture creation courses to take place at the beginning and not at the end of entrepreneurship programs. Students experience the ups and downs of entrepreneurship and learn about the sweat equity associated with a start-up. They gain knowledge of the importance of leadership, yet struggle with finding and developing their own style. They practice entrepreneurship and, through experience, learn about the power of human agency; yet effectively managing and utilizing human resources is more art than science. Students feel defeat after making poor decisions and experience elation over small wins. In hindsight, they underestimate the role of trust between managers and employees and learn delegation is not a choice. In the end, they finally learn that the best opportunity in the world is of little value without a strong team that can execute. Such strength is derived from open and constant communication, shared but challenging goals, and the ability to adapt in uncertain environments.

Serious Games and Simulations

Babson, similar to a few other schools, has been investigating and experimenting with the use of serious games in our entrepreneurship curriculum for some time. To date, our focus has been on three main areas. First, we developed and tested a social media alternative reality game for teaching social media to faculty members.

Another one of our game experiments was the use of an off-the-shelf computer game. The Sims, and the expansion packet, Open for Business. The purpose of the game was to compact the business creation process in order to map the creation of organizational culture, particularly through the way the student / entrepreneur / player used his or her time and his or her money in relation to the business, the employees, and the community.

"IN AN EVER-CHANGING WORLD, WE NEED TO TEACH METHODS THAT STAND THE TEST OF DRAMATIC CHANGES IN CONTENT AND CONTEXT"

Finally, we developed a video game to support learning about how entrepreneurs think under conditions of risk, uncertainty, and unknowability.

Design-Based Learning

The basic argument is that entrepreneurs think, and perhaps act, similar to designers. Design is a process of divergence and convergence requiring skills in observation, synthesis, searching and generating alternatives, critical thinking, feedback, visual representation, creativity, problem-solving, and value creation.

In a traditional business plan course, very little time is given to practicing tools of creativity and idea generation. Overall, very little is done to train a student to think more entrepreneurially and creatively participate in opportunity discovery. We argue that such a discovery process should be grounded in fundamental design principles so students are equipped with tools to not only find opportunities but to also make opportunities (Sarasvathy 2008).[2]

Reflective Practice

The idea of encouraging reflection is certainly not new, and if anything, is regaining its currency as a critical component of the overall learning experience.

When reflecting, one considers an experience that has happened and tries to understand or explain it, which often leads to insight and deep learning—or ideas to test on new experiences.

Reflection is particularly important for perplexing experiences, working under conditions of high uncertainty, and problem-solving. As a result, it should not be a surprise that reflection is an integral component of entrepreneurship education and also a way of practicing entrepreneurship.

A primary objective of reflection is deep learning. Marton (1975) categorized learning as surface or deep.[3] Surface learning is associated with a more passive approach that is premised on a model of education that is dependent on learning, absorbing, and regurgitating. Deep learning is associated with a more active approach characterized by a desire to grasp and synthesize information for valuable and long-term meaning.

Conclusions

There is agreement, at least in theory but not in practice, that entrepreneurship courses should be taught differently from the traditional management courses (Vesper and McMullen 1988).[4]

[2] Sarasvathy, S. D. (2008). *Effectuation: Elements of Entrepreneurial Expertise*. Cheltenham: Edward Elgar.
[3] Marton, F. (1975). "What Does It Take to Learn?" in *How Students Learn*. Eds. N. Entwistle and D. Hounsell. Lancaster: Institute for Research and Development in Post Compulsory Education, 125–138.
[4] Vesper, K.H. and W.E. McMullen (1988). 'Entrepreneurship: Today Courses, Tomorrow Degrees?' *Entrepreneurship Theory and Practice*, 13(1), 7-13.

The method approach is teachable, learnable, but it is not predictable. Starting businesses help students "feel" what it is like to assume the role of an entrepreneur. Serious games and simulations allow students to play in virtual worlds that mirror reality. Designer-based learning encourages students to observe the world through a different lens and create opportunities. Finally, reflective practice gives permission to our students to take time, think, and absorb the learning of their practice-based curriculum.

Together, our portfolio of feeling, playing, observing, creating, and thinking is the entrepreneurship method and a prescription for practice. The method is people dependent but not dependent on a type of person. The entrepreneurship method goes beyond understanding, knowing, and talking and demands using, applying, and acting.

Most importantly, the method requires practice. Entrepreneurship requires practice. Learning a method, in our opinion, is often more important than learning specific content. In an ever changing world, we need to teach methods that stand the test of dramatic changes in content and context. At the end of the day, perhaps we do not teach entrepreneurship the discipline. Perhaps we teach a method to navigate the discipline.

Neck

structured

chaos

experi

fearless

the entrepreneurial college

An article by

Fintan Donohue

Principal / CEO, North Hertfordshire College

A new century, a new paradigm, a new college

Dick Palmer Richard Thorold Tom Bewick

❝ WE ARE TRANSFORMING OUR COLLEGES TO DELIVER A NEW MODEL OF EDUCATION FOR A NEW TYPE OF STUDENT ❞

The phrase 'public sector entrepreneurship' will strike some people as a contradiction in terms. It has, however, been the subject of enquiry and debate for over thirty years. Peter Drucker, as long ago as 1985, declared the incorporation of entrepreneurial management into public sector organisations to be "the foremost political task of this generation":[1]

> "The knowledge is there. The need to innovate is clear. They now have to learn how to build entrepreneurship and innovation into their own system. Otherwise, they will find themselves superseded by outsiders..." (pp.168-169)

Several decades later, entrepreneurship is still seen by many as the prerogative of "outsiders"; and the public sector, while needing to innovate to deliver excellent services in a rapidly changing world, remains risk-averse. But there are public sector leaders who are not risk-averse; who want to take risks because they want their stakeholders to benefit from new ideas and new technology. And there are leaders in colleges who are willing to accommodate failure because they want their staff and students to be creative without

---

[1] Drucker, P. (1985). *Innovation and Entrepreneurship*. Butterworth-Heinemann, Oxford.

141

fear of reproval. While we know that we won't bankrupt our organisations in the legal sense we must, nevertheless, be fearful of leaving an even more damaging legacy of non-delivered services and limited opportunities as a result of a bankruptcy of ideas and innovation.

"IT IS ABOUT ENGENDERING THE CREATIVE SPIRIT IN OUR STUDENTS—ABOUT SAYING IT'S OK TO FAIL BECAUSE IT'S OK TO TAKE RISKS"

The Prime Minister recently launched StartUp Britain, an initiative run by and for entrepreneurs to inspire and accelerate an enterprise-led economic recovery. Like its US equivalent, the Startup America Partnership, it has brought successful entrepreneurs and corporations together to galvanise nascent entrepreneurs and support them on the road to commercial success. This is an important and exciting new initiative; but public sector entrepreneurs do not yet have a high profile at this type of ground-breaking event.

The StartUp Britain campaign plans to provide support to colleges and students by way of entrepreneurial mentors and private sector initiatives. We all welcome this but contend that it is not always necessary to look to "outsiders"—to the private sector—to provide the innovative thinking, financing and proactive risk-taking needed to transform the sector. Private sector organisations already deliver a large share of publicly funded adult education with many predicting that the 'private university' will soon be followed by the 'private college'. There is evidence that progressive approaches to work-based delivery are more often found in private training enterprises. They are free of the constraints that accompany the operation of a more complex organisation such as a college. It was hardly surprising, therefore, that the growth and success of the Newcastle College Group was facilitated, in part, by the takeover of Carter & Carter Group plc, a large private sector training company. But that decision—that entrepreneurialism—came from within the public sector. The college determined the nature of the relationship with the private sector and integrated it into the public sector on their own terms and in support of their own stakeholders.

One of the most iconic phrases in entrepreneurship theory is Joseph Schumpeter's "creative destruction" which calls for the destruction of the old to make way for the new. Carl J. Schramm, the President and CEO of the Marion Ewing Kauffman Foundation, prefers a more benevolent approach to change which he calls "subversive reconstruction":[2]

> "And how is subversive reconstruction accomplished? By hard work. In part, by setting examples through pilot or prototype programs that turn out so well that others are compelled to follow. In part, by networking and educating. In part, by being persuasive in a friendly way, but also by not fearing to step on some toes and point out the obvious when that is called for. And, ultimately, by having the right kinds of ideas to begin with." (pp.14-15)

This is change from within and while we have the skills—the desire, the networks, the courage and the "right kinds of ideas"—we question the likelihood of success when the very culture, modus operandi and historical ethos of public education is antipathetic to change; when "time horizons are short but institutional response times are long".[3] We need a new model—a new paradigm—that goes beyond entrepreneurial mentors and applied private sector support and that is about more than 'shared services'. We need to generate our own private entities, defined and governed by us, but with the freedom and agility to 'step on the toes' of bureaucracy and transform our colleges to deliver a new model of education for a new type of student in an increasingly transformed workplace.

This reflects the view of a pioneering group of individuals who believe this is where we need to be to compete on level terms with the largest private sector providers.[4] College leaders tend to be some of the most entrepreneurial public sector leaders in the country; but their institutions are not inherently entrepreneurial. They were created to provide

---

[2] Kauffman *Thoughtbook 2011* (www.kauffman.org/about-foundation/kauffman-thoughtbook-2011)
[3] Morris, M.H., Jones, F.F. (1999). "Entrepreneurship in established organisations: the case of the public sector" in *Entrepreneurship Theory and Practice*, No.Fall, pp.71-91.
[4] Dick Palmer (City College Norwich), Richard Thorold (Gateshead College), Fintan Donohue (North Hertfordshire College) and Tom Bewick.

qualifications and wider support for communities that, until very recently, enjoyed the prospect of employment within large local organisations such as Vauxhall and Cadbury; organisations that took the welfare of their vast workforces seriously and who looked to colleges to provide a supply of uniformly skilled workers on an annual basis. Sir Ken Robinson argues that this 'industrial model' of education, formulated at the end of the nineteenth century to meet the needs of industrial transformation, is alive and well today and is wholly unsuited to an economy that must compete through knowledge, creativity and innovation:[5]

> "… the growing demand in businesses world-wide is for forms of education and training that develop 'human resources' and in particular the powers of communication, innovation and creativity. This is because of the incessant need for businesses to develop new products and services and to adapt management styles and systems of operation to keep pace with rapidly changing market conditions. Creative abilities are needed in all forms of business and in all types of work including traditional manufacturing and trades. They are also at the centre of some of the most dynamic and rapidly expanding areas of the world economies." (p.19)

It is these "creative abilities" that lie at the core of the entrepreneurial mindset and, as a group, we are reclaiming entrepreneurship as a positive value for the public good. It is about engendering the creative spirit in our students— about saying it's OK to fail because it's OK to take risks. And this is not just about the UK economy—it's about the global economy. There is an increasing recognition of the significance of entrepreneurship across the world as evidenced by the emergence of initiatives such as Global Entrepreneurship Week, Peter Jones' 'Tenner Tycoon' and Michael Furdyk's 'Sprout E-course' online entrepreneurship programme.

We believe that the creation of 'The Entrepreneurial College' requires high levels of resourcing and investment. New entities predicated on a federation aligning innovation, curriculum, technology and growth, would position our colleges as the entrepreneurial hubs of their local communities.[6] New

---

[5] Robinson, Sir K et al. National Advisory Committee on Creative and Cultural Education (May 1999). All Our Futures: Creativity, Culture and Education. Report to the Secretary of State for Education and Employment and the Secretary of State for Culture, Media and Sport.

[6] As Footnote 4 above together with a change management Principals' group from UK colleges.

entities, run by and for the public sector, would embrace the very best of private sector thinking and seek the investment and leadership of entrepreneurs who enjoy the largesse of industry and government. It would employ a limited number of staff who would be recruited purely on their ability to develop and deliver the innovation and transformation that we need but that cannot easily be realised from within the straitjacket of the more traditional sector paradigm.

The Entrepreneurial College will draw on the philosophy and practices of institutions such as the Kauffman Foundation and Babson College; theorists and teachers such as Michael H. Morris and Julian Birkinshaw; and the ideas and work of others in the field, such as Michael Furdyk and Caroline Casey, who have argued for the broader benefits of the entrepreneurial mindset in education and across all three sectors. It will have a clearly defined set of values, will be a visible presence across all our campuses, and the entrepreneurial ethos will be embraced as a strategic driver in all business decisions. Students will learn in an environment that favours experiential learning over the more traditional curriculum model. 'Destination' will be their starting point and success will be measured by employability, self-employment and business start-ups. Entrepreneurship will be defined as much by the value students can add to existing businesses as by their ability to start their own business; and the wider college community, including managers and teachers, will become expert in building and creating successful ventures across the many organisational areas of the college.

The Entrepreneurial College will embrace initiatives such as Global Entrepreneurship Week as a reinforcement of our 'whole college' approach to enterprise. It will not utilise 'bolt on' programmes which, while they may have inherent value, will not add to and may, indeed, detract from the development of the 'whole college' entrepreneurial ethos. For large private colleges in the US, such as Babson, entrepreneurship is considered to be a "way of life"; and in the rarified world of the Ivy League universities there are similarly integrated programmes. Our students won't be paying the £30,000 per annum charged by these luminaries but they will benefit from a learning environment that will apply their philosophies and pedagogies.

'Big Society' is not just about localism. It is about enabling individuals and communities to become more self-sufficient and less dependent upon the state. It is about rolling back the state and increasing choice through deregulation and greater competition in public sector markets. The Entrepreneurial College could be the 'new entrant' in this market place. It would be the catalyst for the kind of subversive reconstruction that the Kauffman Foundation highlights as a vehicle for change. Employers will value its output and students who wish to develop their skills, create a business and give back to society will find an environment that welcomes and inspires them; an environment that, in the words of Ken Robinson, will help them to develop their powers of communication, innovation and creativity to better prepare them for a productive and successful working life.

"Entrepreneurship education is the first and arguably the most important step for embedding an innovative culture in Europe."

Karen Wilson, 2008

Donohue

entrepr

Reading list

Bellone, C. J. & Goerl, G. F. (1992). 'Reconciling public entrepreneurship and democracy'. *Public Administration Review*, 52(2), 130-134.

Bernier, L. & Hafsi, T. (2007). 'The Changing Nature of Public Entrepreneurship'. *Public Administration Review,* 67: 408-533.

Birkinshaw, J. (2010). *Reinventing Management: Smarter choices for getting work done.* John Wiley & Sons Ltd.

Eurobarometer. (2007). 'Entrepreneurship Survey of the EU (25 Member States), United States, Iceland and Norway'.

The Ewing Marion Kauffman Foundation. (2011). 'Rules for Growth: Promoting Innovation and Growth Through Legal Reform'.

The Ewing Marion Kauffman Foundation. (2007). 'On the Road to an Entrepreneurial Economy: A Research and Policy Guide', Version 2.0.

Kane, T. (2010). 'The Importance of Startups in Job Creation and Job Destruction'. The Ewing Marion Kauffman Foundation.

Kanter, R.M. (1997). *Rosabeth Moss Kanter on the Frontiers of Management.* Boston: Harvard Business School.

Kao, J. (1996). *Jamming: The Art and Discipline of Corporate Creativity.* New York: Harper Business.

Linden, R. (1990). *From vision to reality: Strategies of successful innovators in government.* Charlottesville, VA.

Litan, R. (2010). 'Inventive Billion Dollar Firms: A Faster Way to Grow'. The Ewing Marion Kauffman Foundation.

Markides C.C. & Geroski P.A. (2005). *Fast Second: How Companies Bypass Radical Innovation to Enter and Dominate New Markets.* San Francisco: Jossey Bass.

Marton, F. (1975). 'What Does It Take to Learn?' in *How Students Learn.* Eds. N. Entwistle and D. Hounsell. Lancaster: Institute for Research and Development in Post Compulsory Education, 125–138.

Reading list

Mintzberg, H. (1996). 'Managing government, governing management'. *Harvard Business Review*, 74(May-June), 75-83.

Morris, M.H. & Jones, F.F. (1999). 'Entrepreneurship in established organisations: the case of the public sector' in *Entrepreneurship Theory and Practice*, No.Fall, pp.71-91.

Neck, H. M. & Greene, P. G. (2011). 'Entrepreneurship Education: Known Worlds and New Frontiers'. *Journal of Small Business Mnaagement*, pp. 55-70.

Osborne, D. & Gaebler, T. A. (1992). *Reinventing government: How the entrepreneurial spirit is transforming the public sector*. Reading, MA: Addison-Wesley.

Ramamurti, R. (1986). 'Public entrepreneurs: Who they are and how they operate'. *California Management Review*, 28(3), 142-158

Sarasvathy, S. D. (2008). *Effectuation: Elements of Entrepreneurial Expertise.* Cheltenham: Edward Elgar.

Savage, R. L. (1978). 'Policy Innovativeness as a Trait of American States', *Journal of Politics*, 40 (1978), 212-24.

Stangler, D. (2009). 'The Economic Future Just Happened'. The Ewing Marion Kauffman Foundation.

Tapscott, D & Williams A.D. (2010). *Macrowikinomics: Rebooting business and the world,* Portfolio.

Tapscott, D. (2009). *Grown up Digital: How the net generation is changing your world,* McGraw-Hill.

Tapscott, D & Williams A.D. (2006). *Wikinomics: How mass collaboration changes everything*, Portfolio.

orate

Biographies

Julian Birkinshaw

Julian Birkinshaw is a Full Professor in the Department of Strategic and International Management at the London Business School. He is Co-Founder and Research Director of the Management Lab (MLab).

His main area of expertise is in the strategy and management of large multinational corporations, and on such specific issues as corporate entrepreneurship, innovation, subsidiary-headquarters relationship, knowledge management, network organisations, and global customer management. He is the author of ten books, including Giant Steps in Management (2007), Inventuring: Why Big Companies Must Think Small (2003), Leadership the Sven-Goran Eriksson Way (2002), and Entrepreneurship in the Global Firm (2001), and over fifty articles in such journals as Harvard Business Review and Sloan Management Review.

In 1998 the leading British Management magazine Management Today profiled Professor Birkinshaw as one of six of the "Next Generation of Management Gurus". He is regularly quoted in international media outlets, including CNN, BBC, The Economist, the Wall Street Journal, and The Times.

www.london.edu

Caroline Casey

Caroline Casey is the founder of Kanchi (formerly The Aisling Foundation) and the O2 Ability Awards and is also an international speaker and adventurer. A social entrepreneur, Caroline sits on the board for several government, business and not-for-profit organisations.

Since setting up The Aisling Foundation in 2000, with the aim of enhancing the relationship between disability and society, Caroline has received several high profile awards in recognition of her work worldwide. She was the first Irish person to be appointed a Young Global Leader of the World Economic Forum in 2006 and was awarded an honorary doctorate from NUI Ireland in the same year. In 2006 she also became the first Ashoka fellow from Ireland and the UK and received the Eisenhower Fellowship. A former management consultant with Accenture, Caroline is visually impaired to the degree that she is registered as legally blind.

www.kanchi.org

Martin Doel, OBE

Martin Doel is Chief Executive of Association of Colleges, an organisation that champions and promotes the work of colleges and ensures that they are recognised as major contributors to the economic and social prosperity of the nation. He was formerly Director of Training and Education at the Ministry of Defence, responsible for training and education policy and strategy across all three armed forces including cross Government liaison. He was responsible at Board level for developing HR and training strategy for the Royal Air Force's 45,000-strong workforce, and for delivering training in leadership and management to officers of all three UK services and to those from 47 other nations. Prior to this he held a range of HR, training and intelligence appointments, having first joined the RAF in 1980.

He was appointed OBE in 1998 in recognition of his work in support of operations in the Balkans and his contribution to Anglo-German relations.

www.aoc.co.uk

Biographies

Fintan Donohue

Fintan Donohue is Principal and CEO of North Hertfordshire College. He has a degree in Law and an MPhil in Change Management and has worked extensively in the private sector as an adviser on organisational development and change management. He is an experienced Board member, having held ten non-executive posts since 1990. He is an elected member of both the Learning and Skills Improvement Service (LSIS) Council and the Association of Colleges (AoC) Board of Corporation. As an adviser to the London Organising Committee of the Olympic Games and the Home Office on the Bridging the Gap Olympic Games project, he is at the forefront of a changed agenda for the FE sector.

He is the author of several published articles on leadership, creativity and learner-led organisational development and was the lead Principal adviser to BECTA on technology and innovation for leaders in the public sector. He has most recently published research on the personalisation of leadership in the FE sector. He is an AoC Skills Champion for several industries and is the first Principal in the sector to be appointed FE Ambassador to a Sector Skills Council. His most recent work on the role of entrepreneurship in a changing public sector is breaking new ground and is challenging those who lead in the further education sector to reinvent their curricula for a different future.

www.nhc.ac.uk

Dame Jackie Fisher

Jackie Fisher is Chief Executive of Newcastle College Group, comprising Newcastle College, Skelmersdale and Ormskirk College and The Intraining Group - a national organisation meeting the training and employability needs of employers and employees across the UK.

She is also a Director of Newcastle Gateshead Initiative, a tourism and conferencing organisation; a Director of Business and Enterprise North East, which delivers business support services; a regional council member of the Confederation of British Industry (CBI) and a trustee of two charitable trusts; the Northern Rock Foundation and the Centre for Life.

Jackie was made a Dame in 2010 in recognition of her outstanding contribution to Further Education and Training across the UK.

www.ncgrp.co.uk

Michael Furdyk

Michael Furdyk is the Co-founder and Director of Technology for TakingITGlobal.org, a global online community for young people, providing a platform for millions of youth across more than 200 countries to engage with social issues. Along with managing the technology team at TakingITGlobal, Michael was involved in developing the TIGed education program, and has spoken to over 50,000 educators about the importance of engaging students and integrating technology and global perspectives into the classroom. In 2008, he was named by Contribute Magazine as one of 10 Tech Revolutionaries Redefining the Power and Face of Philanthropy.

www.tigweb.org

Lord Hall of Birkenhead, CBE

Tony Hall was appointed Chief Executive of the Royal Opera House in 2001. He is on the Board of the London Organising Committee for the Olympic Games 2012 and is Chair of the Cultural Olympiad Board. He was formerly Director and then Chief Executive of BBC News and Current Affairs from 1989-2001 and had previously worked in various editorial and production roles for the Corporation. He oversaw the establishment of the BBC News website and new radio stations and television channels including Radio 5 Live, BBC Parliament and BBC News 24. He continues his work in broadcasting as Non-Executive Director of the Channel 4 Corporation and has also chaired a series of reviews for government departments including DCSF and the MoD.

www.roh.org.uk

Peter Jones, CBE

Peter Jones is a prominent entrepreneur and television celebrity with a mission to vastly improve enterprise education in Britain. He has built a £200 million empire as owner, chairman and investor in various businesses ranging from telecoms and leisure to publishing and media.

He started his own telecommunications business in 1998 and by the end of the second year had achieved revenue totalling £44m. In 2001, he was named as Emerging Entrepreneur of The Year by The Times/Ernst & Young, and since 2005 has been a regular judge on BBC2's 'Dragons' Den' show. In 2009, he founded the National Enterprise Academy (NEA); the UKs first non-profit educational institution dedicated to teaching enterprise and entrepreneurship primarily to young people.

www.thenea.org

Michael H Morris

Michael H. Morris holds the N. Malone Mitchell Chair in Entrepreneurship at Oklahoma State University and is head of the university's School of Entrepreneurship.

He formerly held the Chris J. Witting Chair in Entrepreneurship in the Whitman School of Management at Syracuse University. In addition, he has led entrepreneurship programmes that have been ranked consistently among the top ten by U.S. News and World Report, Fortune Small Business, and the Princeton Review/Entrepreneur Magazine. A widely published author and researcher, he has written seven books and more than 100 peer-reviewed academic articles.

www.spears.okstate.edu

Geoff Mulgan

Geoff Mulgan is Chief Executive of the Young Foundation, an organisation dedicated to bringing together insights, innovation and entrepreneurship to meet social needs. During the second half of the 20th century, Michael Young was one of the world's most creative and influential social thinkers and doers, helping to shape the UK's new welfare state and dozens of organisations including the Open University and the Consumers' Association.

Geoff formerly worked in the UK Prime Minister's office and Cabinet Office and before that was the founding director of the think-tank Demos. He is a Visiting Professor at LSE, UCL, Melbourne University and the China Executive Leadership Academy. His latest book is The Art of Public Strategy: Mobilising Power and Knowledge For the Common Good

www.youngfoundation.org

Heidi Neck

Heidi Neck is the Jeffry A. Timmons Professor of Entrepreneurial Studies at Babson College. She is the Faculty Director of the Babson Symposium for Entrepreneurship Educators (SEE) where she passionately works to improve the pedagogy of entrepreneurship education because venture creation is the economic growth engine of society. Her research interests include social entrepreneurship, entrepreneurship education, and creativity.

She has published numerous book chapters, research monographs, and refereed articles in such journals as Journal of Small Business Management, Entrepreneurship Theory & Practice, and International Journal of Entrepreneurship Education. She is on the editorial board of Entrepreneurship Theory & Practice and Academy of Management Learning & Education.

www3.babson.edu

Jonathan Ortmans

Leading the development of Global Entrepreneurship Week on behalf of the Ewing Marion Kauffman Foundation, Jonathan Ortmans has worked to align more than 100 countries to inspire, connect, mentor and engage the next generation of entrepreneurs. In doing so, he has helped assemble an informal coalition of more than 18,000 organizations dedicated to stimulating entrepreneurial activity.

Ortmans brings a wealth of experience to the project, serving as a senior fellow at the Kauffman Foundation. Principally, he advises the Foundation on its global footprint and its interface with policymakers through the Policy Dialogue on Entrepreneurship (hosted at www. entrepreneurship. org). Currently, he also serves as president of the Public Forum Institute, an independent, nonpartisan, not-for-profit organization that enjoys strong bi-partisan congressional support in fostering public discourse on major issues of the day.

www.unleashingideas.org   www.kauffman.org

Andy Raynor

Andy Raynor is Chief Executive and a member of the RSM Tenon Group PLC Board. He joined RSM Tenon on the acquisition of the independent partnership formerly known as BDO Stoy Hayward – East Midlands, where he was managing partner. In almost twenty years with that business he established the corporate finance department and held overall responsibility for business development. During his time with the practice the business grew tenfold.

www.rsmtenon.com

Geoff Russell

Geoff Russell is Chief Executive of the Skills Funding Agency, having previously been the Chief Executive of the Learning and Skills Council. He was tasked with stabilising the LSC and managing its orderly wind down into its two successor bodies: The Skills Funding Agency and the Young Peoples' Learning Agency.

He joined KPMG in Toronto in 1982, moved to the UK in 1988, and in 2002 transferred to KPMG International, working for the Global Chairman as the Head of Practice Development. He accepted a two year secondment to HM Treasury in 2005 as Director of Financial Management Change, responsible for developing and implementing financial management policy across Whitehall. Following his time at HMT, he helped develop financial management solutions for KPMG's Government Advisory Practice, before retiring to offer his private and public sector experience to government.

www.skillsfundingagency.bis.gov.uk